THE PEABODY LIBRARY
Columbia City, Indiana

818
Con

Considine, Robert Bernard
They rose above it

THEY ROSE ABOVE IT

They Rose Above It
The Remarkable Life of Dr. Armand Hammer
Toots
It's All News to Me
It's the Irish
Ripley, the Modern Marco Polo
The Men Who Robbed Brinks
Ask Me Anything—Our Adventures with Khrushchev
(*with W. R. Hearst, Jr. and Frank Coniff*)
Dempsey
Christmas Stocking
Man Against Fire
Panama Canal
Innocents at Home
The Maryknoll Story
The Babe Ruth Story
(*with Babe Ruth*)
General Wainwright's Story
(*with General Jonathan Wainwright*)
Where's Sammy
(*with Sammy Schulman*)
Thirty Seconds over Tokyo
(*with Captain Ted W. Lawson*)
MacArthur the Magnificent
The Rape of Poland

THEY ROSE ABOVE IT

*True stories about men, women and children
who fought back in the face of pain, doubt
and dismay*

By Bob Considine

*Doubleday & Company, Inc.
Garden City, New York
1977*

Library of Congress Cataloging in Publication Data

Considine, Robert Bernard, 1906–1975
   They rose above it.

   1. Biography—20th century.   2. Courage.
I. Title.
CT120.C66   920'.02
ISBN: 0-385-11378-1
Library of Congress Catalog Card Number 75–21221

There is a certain blend of courage, integrity, character and principle which has no satisfactory dictionary name but has been called different things at different times in different countries.

Our American name for it is guts.

LOUIS ADAMIC (1899–1951)

THEY ROSE ABOVE IT

Ahem . . .

It helps when you write about braver souls who have known pain, and given that Devil the old eyeball-to-eyeball confrontation, to have experienced some pain yourself. Even though it is only a pain in the ass.

My problem whenever I'm in the throes of pain, which is embarrassingly infrequent, is that it makes all my friends happy. Nearly everybody who comes to see me during my periodic periods of inertness bursts out laughing instead of reaching for a dry edge of my crying towel. I am incapable of arousing sympathy.

It's the *kind* of accidents I have, I guess.

For example: Did you ever fall into an elevator shaft on the U.S.S. *Hornet* in full view of the President of the United States on the day astronauts Neil Armstrong, Buzz Aldrin and Michael Collins returned from man's first voyage to the moon? No?

I did.

The fabled spacemen were not permitted to leave their helicopter after it had fished them out of the central Pacific and deposited them safely on the carrier's deck. Instead, the chopper was towed to Elevator No. 1 and lowered to the hangar deck, where a large portable aluminum pest-house awaited them. For the next twenty-one days they would be isolated inside it and a larger isolation ward at the Manned Space Center in Houston for fear that they might be carrying lunar bacteria that would scoff at Earth's greatest antibiotics, a shot of whiskey and a couple of aspirins.

The moment Elevator No. 1 sank from the *Hornet*'s flight deck, a bullhorn on the bridge bawled, "Members of the White House party, special guests and the media, go to Elevator No. 2. Immediately!"

God must have bigger things in mind for me than to make me proficient at running like a streak to Elevator No. 2 on an aircraft carrier named after a particularly villainous insect. Anyway, the platform, normally used for raising and lowering jet fighters, was largely filled with White House guests and reporters when I arrived at its edge—the last to arrive. Worse, it was sinking toward the hangar deck.

"Jump for it," a pal—I think—yelled. I jumped toward the sinking deck. At least, the first part of the exercise could be called a jump. What I didn't know is that when a carrier elevator descends —and they descend with the speed of a shot duck—they automatically raise a wire-cable fence around the big hole in the flight deck, for safety's sake.

It tripped me, and I went into a racing dive with the nightmarish feeling that I was diving into an empty pool. I caught up with it, thanks to being overweight, and hit it with a loud kerplunk. The impact knocked my notes all over the windy place, put a dent in my camera, cut my left leg and both wrists (it was a three-point landing), and convinced me not to enlist in the Navy in World War III. Bloodied and bowed, I got up when Elevator No. 2 came to a grinding stop on the hangar deck, and was able to cover the wordless transfer of the Apollo 11 crew from their chopper—dressed in green fatigues and science-fiction masks—to what turned out to be their useless detention.

President Nixon, understandably, displayed no interest in my plunge, even though I had a distant cousin who voted for him. He was reading over the ad lib remarks he would make to the moon men by means of a communications system that reached from just outside their pest-house through a plate-glass window and into their hearing range.

It was a dialogue that made me forget I was bleeding. The President declared that what the men had achieved was the greatest event since the creation of the world. He continued for a bit along the same exalted line, but suddenly and unexpectedly ran out of words. We all stood nearby, pencils poised over notebooks, microphones silently breathing dead air. Then the President resumed.

"How about that All-Star Game?" he asked with boyish enthusiasm. "The National League did it again, right? I think that makes it six out of the last eight for them. But let's not take anything away from those American Leaguers. They're good, too."

The astronauts, who had been orbiting or walking on the *moon* during the ballgame, looked through their window, dumbfounded.

"I guess we were a little too busy to follow the game," Aldrin said. So Nixon described it at some length. Maybe it was the result of my fall, but I suddenly had an eerie feeling that time had reversed itself and I had been flung back through the ages to the day in 1295 when Marco Polo returned to Venice after seventeen years at the court of the Kublai Khan. An excited Venetian sports fan embraces him, before he can say a word about his incredible voyage, and gives him a rundown on the bocci-ball finals between Padua and Verona.

Whatever, several weeks after the episode on the *Hornet* I entered a New York hospital for a general checkup. An unusual diagnosis was made on me while I was undergoing that most abysmal of probes called a proctoscopy. The proctologist, a fine man who took up that profession after flunking his well-digging exam, paused in the middle of the dreadful exercise and exclaimed, "Aha! You've got phlebitis in your left leg!" I still question whether he had probed quite that far. But I did indeed have the phlebitis at the points where I hit the deck of Elevator No. 2. Attendants promptly wrapped my leg until I resembled Henry VIII with a bad case of gout. I was sternly warned that if I took as much as one step toward the bathroom—no matter what the urgency—one or more of my clots would spring loose and shoot me fatally through the heart, lungs and brain.

Those who came to see me in the hospital as the clots were dissolving laughed a great deal. The thought of my falling into the shaft of Elevator No. 2 on the day of the triumphant return from the moon of the completely unscathed crew of Apollo 11 was just too much for them. "Let's face it," one of my best friends said, mid laughter he couldn't suppress, "you've always been a clumsy son of a bitch."

Think that was funny? Well, in the spring of 1975 I hit a mountain in a free balloon . . .

Between gales of hearty laughter by visitors who came to see me in three hospitals, ran the broad theme of, "You must be some kind of a nut," or, "Just like I always said, you're full of hot air," or, "I don't believe it—*you* in a balloon."

I couldn't believe it either. It was my first balloon ride. Might make a good column, I figured: grand view of Lake Tahoe, home movie shots of the snow-crested Sierra Madres, shots of the beautiful high-altitude golf course near the Hyatt hotel (the starting place of the "race"), the magic of silent flight, and the oneness I would share with the eighteenth-century inventors of the stunning device —Joseph and Jacques Étienne Montgolfier and the twentieth century's Malcolm Forbes.

All went well for an hour aloft. But then the young pilot, who was the only other aeronaut in our wicker basket, did something vaguely disturbing: he handed me a crash helmet. The winds we were flirting with around Mount Rose were becoming a bit alarming. We'd breeze along with them for a time, then hang dead in the sky, then press onward or upward or downward, captives of the wind's whims.

One zephyr, against which we were totally helpless, dumped us into the top of a giant pine. The weight of the basket caused the whole clumsy apparatus to begin falling bumpily through breaking or parting limbs. The needles and small branches ripped the bulging fabric of the fat envelope and jabbed like knives through the open patterns of our basket. It was like being mugged by the Jolly Green Giant. But the young pilot pumped fresh flame up into the wounded bag, pushed aside some restraining boughs, and we tore loose.

It might have been better to have stayed in the tree like the Tarzans, *pére et fils*. But that was not to be. Once free of it, the wind took over strongly. The ripped envelope, leaking like a hot-air presidential candidate, rushed us over a mountain road and slammed us against a rocky embankment that rose from the road.

It was by all odds the hardest bump of my life, which has included being hit by a car when I was a dear little apple-cheeked schoolboy who couldn't tell the difference between a red and a green light, and one particularly painful fall from a barstool some years later.

The young balloon pilot was unscratched. Maybe he had rehearsed landings like this one. I? Well, I rattled around and around on the floor of the basket like an overstuffed bean in an oversized maraca. There is a stubbornly enduring myth that your whole life flashes before your eyes in the split second before you face your co-Maker. Rot! The only thing I remember thinking was, "What the hell am I doing in a goddam free balloon in Nevada?" I was sure my back was broken, and for a time I was too frightened to test whether it was—particularly after I heard an early arrival at the crash scene say, "Don't move him."

In time, I was carried down the mountain on a stretcher and lifted into an ambulance which state troopers had ordered sent from the Washau Medical Center in Reno.

"Top-heavy, isn't he?" one stretcher bearer said to another as I was rolled into the ambulance. Upon arrival at that splendid new haven for the maimed, I was wheeled to the pediatrics section of Emergency. None of a series of nurses indicated that they thought I was suffering from colic, but all seemed curious about my mother's maiden name and whether or not I wore contact lenses.

Like a fool, I signed myself out of this splendid care at Washau after a few days and flew to San Francisco. I wanted to continue with my original plan of seeing some of our grandchildren. I managed to get into pajamas, groped my way to a luxurious king-sized bed at a Hyatt hotel . . . and experienced for a couple of days the most excruciating pain of my life. (I held to that conviction until my wife Millie, who may have heard my complaint once too often, said, "Try having a baby sometime, buster.")

My beef against the beautiful bed in San Francisco was that it was not equipped with a simple trapeze device, apparently invented by some unsung monkey, which enables the bed-ridden to reach up, grab the bar for support, and thus raise themselves, lower themselves, or turn over. It costs about two bucks but for those who have ever needed it to avoid becoming a rooted vegetable, it's the greatest invention since the wheel. It gave mobility to the two-by-two-foot bruise on my behind.

I hit a couple more hospitals after Reno, both in New York and both fine, then spent a month at home in a rented hospital bed equipped with the newest model nonskid trapeze bar.

Pretty dull stuff when compared to the immensely more realistic and important tales we'll tell in this little book. But I cannot in good conscience dismiss my own trivial problems without making at least a passing reference to doctors, nurses and enemies of pain in general. It is abundantly true that if the human race were suddenly deprived of them and the fruits of their laboratories, planet Earth would be depopulated even before Big Brother is scheduled to take over in 1984. God bless 'em. Still, I wonder if anybody who has needed their skills shares my crazy feeling that, now and then at least, they regard their patients as wholly unworthy of their patience.

I discovered that it took a certain amount of moxie to press my bedside button in the dead of night to arouse a nurse to help me with a sprung whalebone in my traction corset. I was sure that the bell or light did not activate the nurse but interrupted a meeting in which Henry Kissinger, Anwar Sadat, Yitzhak Rabin and Fatso Arafat were signing a Middle East agreement. The nurse, upon arriving confirmed my fears with a trace of a frown.

I have learned lately to like doctors. I wish doctors liked doctors. With the possible exception of an actor listening to someone speaking warmly of the genius of another actor, no skilled technician can stiffen up stiffer than a doctor forced to hear a patient say a kind word about another doctor, particularly a younger doctor.

"Who ordered this man off Orinase, nurse?" one of my seven doctors thundered after glancing over my chart on his return from a slow-boat trip to the People's Republic of China.

6

The poor woman in white gasped, as so many do when asked such prying questions as, "How's my temperature, sweetie, since your chum took it seven minutes ago?" She finally whispered the name of the anti-Orinase doctor and explained piteously that he had based his decision on an article in *The New York Times* quoting a spokesman of the Federal Drug Administration as saying that Orinase may be a good stopper for diabetes but may cause heart attacks.

"Nonsense!" the doctor in attendance decreed, his WIN button giving off sparks. "Who'd believe anything he read in *The New York Times?* Give this man *four* Orinase tablets a day!"

Doc-3 ordered me back on two tablets a day. I couldn't feel the difference. Doc-4 thought I had a cracked vertebra, Doc-5 laughed at that diagnosis. Doc-6 marched in one day and found me immersed in newspaper clippings about the balloon caper and a lot of letters—including one from General Jimmy Doolittle saying, "If you stay out of my business, I'll stay out of yours," and a nice note on the pale avocado stationery of 1600 Pennsylvania Avenue, Washington, D.C., reading, "Betty and I were saddened to learn of the accident . . . With warm regards, Jerry Ford."

Doc-6 twirled his stethoscope and said briskly, "Well! What brings *you* here?"

I told him I had been shot in a gun duel in a Reno bordello. He wouldn't have believed the balloon story anyway.

Doc-7 was my favorite. His distinguished predecessors had agreed on one point: the impact of hitting Mount Rose produced some gizzard disorders that ruled out forevermore the joy and relaxation of having a modest drink before breakfast, lunch, tea, dinner and bedtime. Doc-7 came in, said hello, took the pin out of his lapel carnation, punched it into the pad of one of my typing fingers, blotted the bead of blood with a tiny square of gauze, looked at it for a good one-fifth of a second, turned to my wife and said, "His blood sugar is okay. Give him a drink and see to it that he gets a lot of fatty foods for his liver."

But now to nittier grittier matters . . . and people.

You may find a knight or two in shining armor in this book, but please tolerate them. They slipped in through a side door. Perhaps the publisher failed to notify them that this book is devoted largely to the heroism and stoicism of persons who were not born with silver swords in their mouths, not lumpy with great muscles—just people who discovered in themselves a measure of majesty they may not have known they possessed when the chips were stacked against them. People like you, let's say.

I accumulated these stories at first hand or learned the details from responsible reporters during a life that, at times, seems to reach back to the invention of movable type. Roosevelt's ". . . a day that will live in infamy"; Churchill's ". . . finest hour" and MacArthur's "I shall return" are declarations that will raise goose bumps on the hides of schoolchildren a thousand years hence. But they have no particular role here. My pantheon is as prosaic as the guy next door, or at the other end of the ward. Those who fill its niches do not have togas. Their names are names you hear at work, names like Ted, Jim, Doc, Mildred, Rosemary, Barney, Lou, Eddie, Jack—even Sister.

Sister?

Might as well start with her. She had something to say on the spur of an unnerving moment that may run like a brave little thread through the psyches of all the others.

Chapter 1

Courage is grace under pressure.

ERNEST HEMINGWAY (1899–1961)

The dashingly uniformed U.S. war correspondent, redolent with an overdose of PX Aqua Velva, stepped warily into a primitive Chinese field hospital during the early days of World War II. He was offended by the smell of the dead and dying and the incoherent cries of the wounded. Beating a hasty retreat in search of fresh air, he was suddenly nailed in his tracks by an incomprehensible sight:

A young and beautiful nun of the American-based Maryknoll order was on her knees patiently swabbing the gangrenous leg of a filthy Chinese soldier lying on a reeking mat. The correspondent turned his gaze away in revulsion.

"Sister," he said, "I wouldn't do that for a million dollars."

The nun momentarily paused in her ministrations of the badly wounded man, and said:

"Neither would I."

Chapter 2

Old men have need to touch sometimes with their lips the cheek of a child, that they may believe again in the freshness of life.

MAURICE MAETERLINCK (1862–1949)

Young women, too, as well as old men. Young women like Rosemary Taylor. She is a lovely Australian girl who has weathered difficulties and at least one major disaster whose accumulated emotional effect might have turned a bronze lioness to jelly.

There is need for a preface before Maeterlinck's words stick together:

I first met Rosemary at Phu My, a creaky old French-built hospital-orphanage in the Cholon slums of Saigon. She looked like a virginal Elizabeth Taylor. I met her through Colonel George Hennrikus, USAF, a good man who like many others in the American military tried to keep alive the desperately needed Vietnamese orphanages with whatever they could beg, borrow or scrounge. Phu My was (and probably remains) a distressing place overly filled with infants and young children deposited at its gate in dead of night or rounded up by volunteers like Rosemary in gutters and on garbage heaps. Derelicts, too.

Rosemary was something to behold, miraculously immaculate in the wailing chaos and squalor of a war that still had years to run. She seemingly worked 'round the clock, without feeling "beat," for any inmate of Phu My who was too old to live or too young to die. She had a special therapy for both, in addition to all the standard remedies, if such were available. She would play a soft guitar for them at night, waiting for an all-but-nonexistent doctor to arrive, and sing them a lullaby. But Rosemary was more than a madonna with her jet-black hair held in tow by a spotless white headband.

She could leap from the side of a sick child's cot and, swinging her precious guitar like a broadax, rout thieves so desperate they had climbed a wall to steal whatever they could lift—even the soiled diapers of abandoned infants.

"Doesn't the South Vietnamese Government help you keep this place going?" I asked her after her heroic efforts to hold Phu My together during the Tet offensive of 1968.

"Yes," she said without visible anger. "They give us four cents a day for each child. Nothing for the old people."

Yet, in face of such appalling odds, Rosemary Taylor put together and operated four orphanage-clinics in Saigon between that time and the surrender of the remnants of the disorganized Thieu forces. Depending on the mood of Washington, she sometimes received surplus food and medicine, sometimes not. For a time she was granted an APO number, later permitted to receive mail and contributions through the U. S. Embassy, and then for no reason was cut off. More substantially endowed charitable organizations such as Colonel and Mrs. Pat Tisdale's An Lac Orphanage, which had been founded in the middle nineteen fifties by the legendary Dr. Tom Dooley and Madam Ngai, a spirited North Vietnamese refugee, kept Rosemary Taylor's operations going when conditions were bleakest. So did the selfless response to her far-flung appeals for volunteers: interns, student nurses, leave-taking nuns, GIs who missed their own kids, and good-hearted American housewives like Constance Boll of peaceful, antiseptic New Canaan, Connecticut.

Rosemary had what amounted to several full-time jobs. If one took precedence over the others, it was her ceaseless task of arranging for the adoption of her children. The same government that could be so cynical in supporting its war-born population explosion could be maddeningly deliberate about letting its lost generation find love, comfort, an education and opportunity with overseas families eager to provide a fresh start, new life. Rosemary spent a numbing portion of her life in Saigon standing in line before some atrociously incompetent or listless bureaucrat's desk or counter seeking visas for her young. There was hardly ever an end to the questioning, the incompetence and the stalling. She was expected to know the names, occupations, age and addresses of parents and relatives of children she did not know existed until she heard their wails at her doorstep. The blizzards of documents she had to fill out were to be done in triplicate. But there was never any carbon paper . . .

Still, she sent or shepherded dozens upon dozens of helpless children to new lands. On more than one occasion when a child died despite all her cares and prayers, just as the baby had been cleared by Saigon to leave the country for its new home, Rosemary would somehow manage to replace the dead baby with a healthy one, give him or her the dead baby's name, and save the new family from weeks and months of new negotiations.

As elsewhere in the world of children, not all of Rosemary's babies were adorable counterparts of petite oriental dolls found in expensive toy stores. Some, whose names never made the casualty lists, were maimed by war. Some were retarded. Some were afflicted with sores that would not heal, faces that were considered too ugly, and some were penalized by the inexorable cruelty of time. They became seven or eight or nine years old and were adopted by Vietnamese families, often as servants, lackeys, and breadwinners at such trades as shoeshining, newspaper selling, and procuring.

One of her special problems was the care and placement of children sired of Vietnamese girls by American black troops.

"The poor dears are given a terrible time, by and large," she told me on one of many visits. "They're terribly discriminated against in the elementary schools, and even in some of the orphanages. Their futures are grim. Even if their mothers kept them and they are now married to Vietnamese husbands and have other children, the stepfathers have no real love for their part-black child. Children their own age ostracize them, call them 'black Americans.' They're the most obvious of the many illegitimate children you see in Saigon and elsewhere in South Vietnam. Some of the children of white American soldiers could easily pass as all-Vietnamese, or even all-white, and I pray they do. But the half-black Vietnamese child is someone apart, no matter how dear the child, how hard it tries to fit in and be loved."

If you knew Rosemary and happened to be returning to the U.S. (or any other country) after an assignment, chances were that you would not travel unaccompanied. You'd take one of her passport-bearing children with you to deliver to the arms of the child's new parents. There was no way to say no to Rosemary. Thus it was that I came to know and fall in love with nineteen-month-old Ngo Thi Lam, phonetically pronounced (most undeservedly) Naughty Lamb. I heard about her as a tender victim of the chaos and callousness of the war. She had been abandoned outside a crowded orphanage in the Can Tho section of the Mekong Delta where, by one chance in a million, she had been seen at six months of age by U. S. Air Force Captain Robert Allen Peck, who had a wife and two young sons back in the States. Touched, he wrote to his good wife Phyllis, living half a world away, and they decided to adopt Naughty Lamb.

The adoption process—permission to leave South Vietnam, passport, papers (in triplicate), etc.—took an excruciating thirteen months. ("Is Ngo Thi Lam, the applicant, a member of the Viet Cong? . . . Why does she wish to leave her native land?") During the long wait, Captain Peck completed his tour of duty and was reassigned to stateside duty, whereupon the task of freeing the baby fell upon the frail-looking but highly resilient shoulders of Rosemary Taylor.

She knew I had booked passage from Saigon to San Francisco the next day, but she also knew that W. R. Hearst, Jr., his son Will, and the Hearst Service's chief European writer, Joseph Kingsbury-Smith, and I had an interview scheduled with Vice President Ky at the palace on this day before our departure. It was to be an interview involving many momentous military and diplomatic events, but Rosemary could not have cared less. "Ask him to light a fire under those nitwits who are holding up Naughty Lamb's 'papers,'" she said. I did at the end of the long interview.

Early the next morning, with still no word from Rosemary or

any member of Ky's staff, I taxied out to what was called "Pentagon East" for an interview with William Colby, who held ambassadorial status as head of our political investment in South Vietnam, and later became director of the Central Intelligence Agency—of which he was probably even then an important but shadowed figure. When I arrived back at the Caravelle Hotel in Saigon, the phone was ringing. It was Rosemary. A miracle had been wrought. Naughty Lamb's papers had arrived! She could go!

I was punching out the Colby interview in my room—his point was, as I recall, that we were winning the war—when there was a knock on my door and Rosemary carried in Naughty Lamb and put her gently down on the spare bed. The quiet little doll with the button nose and the most luminous dark eyes I ever saw just lay there, making no sound as she looked up at the strange ceiling in the only room she had ever known that was not filled with the babbling and weeping of other bereft children. I hurriedly finished my story, called United Press International, and filed it to New York.

There was barely time to scoop up my luggage and close my typewriter. Naughty Lamb was traveling lighter. Her total possessions barely filled a small Air Vietnam airline bag: her formula, disposals, nightgown, socks, panties, toothbrush, hairbrush and comb, and a fresh dress to wear on her arrival in the U.S.

Ton Son Nhut airport was its usual self, a Babel with added tongues, ear-splitting announcements, crushing heat, the thunder of a crazed variety of military and commercial planes landing and taking off, apparently nobody in charge except a girl behind a Mutual of Omaha flight-insurance counter, and a fly in the stifling restaurant's perpetual *soup du jour:* Chinee Soupee. Naughty Lamb, bonnet in place, retained her cool, even when a fluttering covey of French nuns from Phu My sliced through the pandemonium to pick her up and kiss her good-bye. Rosemary carried her to the distant steps of the Air Vietnam Caravelle. We found a seat and she put the baby on my lap. I felt as proud as Whistler's father. We took off between a lumbering C-141 freighter and a rapier-like F-101, cozy in our own little niche in a wretched war.

It seemed like a good time to celebrate. I asked the stewardess to warm up Naughty Lamb's formula and to bring me a scotch and soda. My baby and I sat there contentedly having our contrasting shots until a lively army nurse, on a rest and relaxation furlough, came forward and burst into laughter at the sight of the Odd Couple. "What a picture that would make!" she said, expertly plucking Naughty Lamb off my lap and carrying her through the admiring passengers. It made me feel very proud.

Trouble at Hong Kong upon arrival, late evening. Sort of a case of Her Majesty's Crown Colony vs. Miss Ngo Thi Lam, Vietnamese alien. The baby and I were ticketed to leave on Pan Am the next morning at nine. Everybody in our group had rooms or suites waiting for them to occupy in town . . . everybody except that apparently sinister figure Naughty Lamb, who had brought a dinner roll off the Air Vietnam plane with her and was now daintily offering little bits of it to all who stopped to admire her as she sat on a hard bench in Immigration. She could not be permitted to enter the British enclave because its alien quota was filled! The man in the uniform was quite adamant about it. Orders, he said, were made to be obeyed. And they were indeed, for two exasperating hours, until the Hearsts and Joe Kingsbury-Smith reached higher authority and the suspect baby was sprung, still distributing bits of bread.

About midnight of a strange and probably frightening day that had begun for her in a suffocating ward at Phu My, Naughty Lamb and I purred to the Peninsula Hotel in an air-conditioned Rolls-Royce the Mandarin Hotel had sent to the airport to fetch Bill Hearst. Bill had left it for us and had gone into town balanced on a creaky Mandarin baggage truck. A posh room awaited us at the ornate old Peninsula, a crib for my girl, a bed for me. I mixed her formula, spilling about half of it in the process, changed and washed her with a warm towel. I have four children and, at last count, four grandchildren. But Naughty Lamb remains the only child I have ever changed. I put on her fresh diaper and her nightgown and placed the dear angel in her crib. She must have been utterly exhausted, but there had not been a sound out of her all day and this far into the night.

Sometime around 4 A.M. she sneezed, and I vaulted out of my bed as if the place had been bombed. She was awake. Her nose was running! I rattled the room phone, got the operator, and demanded that the house doctor be roused and sent up immediately. In a few minutes a starched young Chinese nurse appeared. There was no doctor available. She wiped Naughty Lamb's button nose with a Kleenex, changed her, gave her half an aspirin in a thimble of water, rubbed her little back, and the lids and lashes of her beautiful eyes fell like gentle curtains.

An hour or two out of Tokyo, en route to San Francisco where Phyllis Peck would be waiting, Naughty Lamb and I were playing a game she liked. Lying in her airline crib which fitted against the bulkhead of the 707, she would pull a light blanket over her face and then reach out from under it and expose the little finger of her left hand. I would kiss it, pull back the blanket, and find her smiling ever so happily.

But once when I pulled back to the blanket, Naughty Lamb was not smiling. She was silently weeping. Great tears were running down her doll cheeks. I rang for the stewardess, and when she came I asked what was wrong, why the baby was crying but making no crying sound.

The stewardess, an old hand at this phenomenon, I guess, said a most chilling thing:

"I've seen this before with these kids," she said with a shrug. "The reason they don't make any noise when they cry is because they learned a long time ago that nobody will come."

I picked Naughty Lamb out of her crib, held her cheek close to mine, and this waif of a senseless war and I had a nice quiet cry together.

The Pecks gave Ngo Thi Lam a new name: Tiffany Peck. The United States Government census computers know her by that name, too. The U. S. Immigration and Naturalization Service computers, having agreed with findings made by agents over several years of investigation, have concluded that Naughty Lamb is not engaged in prostitution, is not a member of the Communist Party, has no known intention of overthrowing the U. S. Government by force, and would defend her adopted country in time of war against its enemies.

I was there in Phi Beta Kappa Hall, College of William and Mary, Williamsburg, Virginia, when the newest, and perhaps the youngest, naturalized citizen of the United States, five-year-old Miss Peck, raised her hand and repeated, after Professor Eric Fisher: "I believe in the United States of America as a government of the people, by the people, and for the people." I heard her trill along with the vocalist who sang "God Bless America." And, for a little girl, she seemed to pay rapt attention to retired U. S. Supreme Court Justice Tom Clark as he expounded on how some of the Founding Fathers had made that very plot of land sacred by their courageous stand against tyranny.

Rosemary? I gave her such progress reports on Ms. Peck as her variable addresses would permit, raised a little dough for her new babies, met good people who had brought babies here for her, sweated out her never-ending problem of pumping sustenance and hope into her expanding complex: *four* havens. They cost fifteen thousand dollars a month to run in the skyrocketing inflation in which Saigon was immersed.

Then, to what seemed to Rosemary and her brood, an authentic miracle. A sufficient number of hearts had been moved at AID in Washington, the bountiful Agency for International Development. AID announced it would set aside two hundred and fifty thousand dollars a year for Rosemary's operation. It was the Agency's smallest grant, in all probability, but surely its most welcome.

The rest is heartbreak, relieved only by the unquenchable flame of Rosemary's spirit.
—The U.S. troops went home, abandoning hundreds of children.
—The Viet Cong and the North Vietnamese beat AID to Saigon.

17

—Begging and borrowing and selling whatever she owned in a city that had gone berserk with panic, Rosemary arranged to charter a U.S. commercial 747 that could have picked up her four hundred children and their nurses and volunteers and flown the lot to America.

—A man from the airline called at the last moment. Sorry, he said, another refugee organization had offered more money and would get the plane. He hoped Rosemary understood, he added.

—A French charter service called to say it expected a 707 to arrive the next morning, and it would be available. Rosemary ordered it. But Ton Son Nhut airport was bombed that night, so the French plane never arrived.

—Eureka! Someone from AID called. President Ford had become a patron of Operation Baby Lift. Get the babies' "papers" in order, pile everything and everybody in buses, get to Ton Son Nhut as quickly as the chaos of the streets would permit: there was a great big beautiful U. S. Air Force C5-A waiting for them—the biggest plane in the world.

The pandemonium of the air terminal was bypassed. There was no longer any time for protocol. The United States had said this-is-how-it's-going-to-be, see? The children's buses were driven right to the cavernous doors of the incredible cargo plane. The first passenger aboard was not a child. It was the Vietnamese driver of the first bus. The terrified man locked himself in one of the plane's toilets. The Vietnam MPs on hand broke down the door, dragged him off the C5-A screaming, and beat him unconscious with their clubs. Rosemary and her helpers worked with the big jet's crew, arranging the children, the older ones on the lower deck, the infants and very young strapped together—too tightly, she'd remonstrate from time to time—on the upper deck. She tried to kiss everybody good-bye, promised she would see them soon, and waved to the waving hands framed in the tiny ports as the goliath—flagship of the Baby Lift— waddled toward the runway.

Her phone was ringing when she reached her office . . .

Twenty minutes out of Ton Son Nhut the rear ramp and the

pressure door of the huge plane blew their locks and shot off into space, but not before cutting a gaping wound in the fuselage and severing several major control cables. The runway was cleared as the crew gamely fought to bring the gravely wounded ship back to a safe harbor. But hardly more than a mile from where its twenty-eight wheels might have touched down, the C5-A hit and degutted itself. One hundred and fifty-five of the children she had worked so hard to bring this close to adoption—most of them on the bottom deck of the plane—were literally and terribly scraped to death. Nuns, nurses and ordinary people who simply had cared, were also killed and wounded. The main survivors were the babies on the top deck, because they *were* strapped in too tightly.

—A rentable 747 arrived unexpectedly the next day. If she had known it was coming, Rosemary could have taken all the children out safely.
—In time, Senator William Proxmire (D-Wis.) charged that the tragedy of "Baby Lift ⚡1" could be repeated every time a C5-A takes to the air; that the Air Force (which bitterly denied the charge) had been covering up this engineering weakness since the birth of the plane.

For Rosemary, there simply wasn't any time for tears or temperament in her last hours in Saigon. There were children to be buried, injured to be hospitalized, the C5-A litter to be searched for the "papers" and names of the dead and living, properties to be put in the hands of the French, British, Swiss and Australians who had been quick to recognize the victors diplomatically. She found still another 747 charter, a Pan Am, and, even more incredibly, a sponsor who put up two hundred and fifty thousand dollars to send it and its battered children to haven. He was Robert McCauley, a Connecticut corrugated-paper manufacturer who had become interested in Saigon's "Shoe Shine Boys"—bands of homeless youths given shelter, schooling and incentives by a remarkable young U.S. social worker Dick Hughes, who had given up journalism and government service to corral and care for his maverick kids. McCauley provided a plane to get them out of the falling city. When Hughes and his lads voted to stay, come what may, Rosemary inherited the charter. As with other late-departing planes, weeping women young and old carried uncertified and wailing children to the doors of the jammed planes and, when told sternly that no one else could be boarded, simply thrust the children into the nearest offered arms and fled into the mob.

Rosemary escaped, on one of the last helicopters, from what was already being called Ho Chi Minh City, not the Saigon where she had labored for a decade without any thought of pay, or even a thank-you. The chopper's destination was the tiny pad on the stern of the freighter *Blue Ridge,* riding at sea off Saigon. Such was the urge of the *Blue Ridge* to take its refugees aboard and pull anchor that, as each copter and its passengers and crew landed and leaped out on the pad, *Blue Ridge* crewmen would push it into the water to make room for the next helicopter. Awaiting its chance of making it to the pad, the chopper carrying Rosemary began to run out of fuel. It sank so close to the debris-filled water that her feet dangled in the drink. But there was one last burst of power from the engine which enabled the aircraft to reach the pad where, once emptied of its people, it was pushed overboard.

Conditions aboard the *Blue Ridge* were subhuman. When it reached the Philippines, the suffocating refugees were told they could not leave the ship. But the protests were so loud and clear that they were put aboard a somewhat larger hell-ship named *Greenport* for the stifling voyage to Guam.

Rosemary took a day or two off after she reached the comparative peace of headquarters, Friends of All Children (Boulder, Colorado), an organization that had moved mountains to help her thought the latter years of her stay in Vietnam. Close friends who tried to call her by phone were told she was not available or, if they reached her, found her in a state of shock. They understood: in a few short months and on the brink of clear sailing, her life's work, her dreams and prayers for a better world for children, ostensibly abandoned by God and man, had been demolished.

But one morning she woke up, hid her scars, and went back to doing what came so naturally. She returned to the intimidating jig-saw of arranging, as far as humanly possible, the names of the C5-A dead, which had included her closest friend, an Australian class-mate. She must regenerate her correspondence with American, Canadian, European and Australian families who were awaiting the arrival of children they had arranged to adopt—many now dead, some battered for life. She also felt it her duty, that day her sorry sabbatical ended, to start working for the return to Vietnam, as soon as possible, of refugees who had been caught up in the mael-strom of panic in the last days of the war and had found themselves leading difficult and homesick lives in a sometimes hostile new world.

She did not for an instant feel that returnees would return to a bloodbath. Upon reaching the U.S., and having experienced so much grinding trouble with South Vietnamese bureaucracy and budgetary bones thrown to her children from the palace pantry, she told a reporter: "I can't conceive of Saigon becoming another Phnom Penh. I don't know about the religious aspects of the take-over by the Viet Cong and the North Vietnamese, but it can only be good politically, considering what went before."

Rosemary was in New York briefly not long ago, delivering a Vietnamese baby to joyful parents. The baby had survived not only the C5-A debacle but a bad case of vitiation when the rescuing 747 ran out of water and air conditioning while waiting two hours for a busy President Ford to show up be photographed holding one of the children. Rosemary had added a pound and a half to the baby's weight before delivering her.

"What's the baby's name?" I asked Connie Boll, who had alerted me that Rosemary was headed our way on another mission of mercy.

"Turtle Dove," Connie said. "She's one of the last of Rosemary's Vietnamese babies."

What will happen to Rosemary when they're all placed? Connie Boll seemed surprised by the question.

"More of the same, what else?" she answered. "She's got her scouts out. The world is full of orphaned and abandoned kids who need a Rosemary . . . the Philippines, Central and South America, and what about Sri Lanka? Don't worry, you'll be hearing from her . . ."

On the day of the C5-A crash my mind was cluttered with memories of Naughty Lamb, then "going on six." I wired a flowering plant to her home in Virginia, which did little to comfort her that terrible day. But in time she wrote me a thank-you note in her nice block letters to tell me she had transplanted it to the family garden and was watering it daily. I'll always treasure Ms. Peck's salutation. It confirmed Maeterlinck. It read:

DEAR NANNY . . .

Chapter 3

An honest man, close-button'd to the chin,
Broadcloth without, and a warm heart within.
WILLIAM COWPER (1731–1800)

There would be something different about burial of one of the ninety-five children burned to death in the fire that destroyed Chicago's Lady of the Angels parochial school in December 1958. The announcement was made by a shivering young priest at the frozen cemetery where the mass burial services would be held.

"It would be too much of a strain on one family to wait until all the other hearses arrived," the priest half-explained, supervising the balancing of the pathetic white casket on its lowering apparatus.

Then it began to be comprehensible to the handful of family friends and reporters who stood near. The members of one family were coming forth, trodding the imitation grass and grief-stricken. The mother, a short woman whose woolen scarf was a frame for a painting or sculpture of grief only a great master would have attempted, was supported by two larger women who sobbed loudly. But it was not she who commanded the thunderstruck attention of those nearby. It was the father of the dead child.

He had little or no visible face of human skin. He wore a startling leather mask that reached down from his hairline to his sensitive mouth. Out of the right side of the horrid covering, at eye level, protruded what appeared to be a jeweler's eyepiece with a pinpoint opening instead of a full lens. He stood there, erect and silent on the arm of a male member of the mourning party.

The young priest droned into the familiar ritual. I couldn't take my eyes away from the mourner's surrealistic mask. Another priest noted my rude fascination. Above the weeping, the Word, and the marrow-freezing wind, he whispered:

"He just came from the hospital against the doctors' wishes. He had an operation for detached retinas a few days ago. They told him that if he cries at the funeral the salt of his tears will enter the incisions and destroy his sight forever."

There this man stood, surrounded by highly contagious wails, fighting for control of his exposed chin. The liturgy went on and on, mixing as of old the melancholy fact of death with the tender gossamer of a life hereafter. I found myself praying other prayers, that this brave man somehow would not do the most natural thing in the world—let free his blinding tears. I watched his lower jaw. It was not the jaw of a fighter; it was just the jaw of an ordinary man who worked hard, one guessed, and now had been visited by more than the human spirit could endure. Once the chin trembled, briefly, then firmed up, fluttered still again, but recovered.

It was time to go now. The women led the stumbling mother away. The man at the afflicted man's arm escorted him down a narrow line between open graves. His head was high, as if reaching for his breath. His jaw was like a rock.

Chapter 4

My mother was a superior soul
A superior soul was she,
Cut out to play a superior role
in the God-damn bourgeoisie.
D. H. LAWRENCE (1885–1930)

"My mother was the finest human being I ever knew," mused Jack Dempsey, the man several generations of boxing writers called the Manassa Mauler.

"She never weighed more than a hundred, hundred-ten. Blue eyes. Jet-black hair, like mine used to be. She had eleven children, some of us without a midwife, most of us without the horse-and-buggy doctor. I remember him. We didn't have much to do with him because he charged twenty-five cents to deliver a kid or make a sick call. I was five when my brother Bruce was born, and nobody was there to help my mother. She dam' near died. Hemorrhage, I guess.

"I remember the summer after Bruce was born we traveled eighty-five miles by wagon to a place named Creede, a mining town on the edge of the Great Divide. My mother had heard of a chance to make a little money there—my father wasn't any help at the time —so she rounded up some of us, got us to Creede, and opened up a boardinghouse. She took care of Joe, Johnny, Elsie, little Bruce and me. Also the old man and the customers. She took in washing on the side.

"That must have been when I started to know that my mother was a wonderful woman. And one of the unluckiest women alive, I guess.

"I never got tired of a story she used to tell me. She'd put an arm around me and say, 'Harry,' that's what everybody called me then, short for William Harrison Dempsey, 'just a little time before you were born a stranger came to our door. He was selling magazines. I told him I had no money for that sort of thing but he was welcome to come in and have a cool glass of milk. When he left he wanted to pay for the milk. I wouldn't hear of it, naturally. So he gave me a useless, battered old book he was toting. It was all about John L. Sullivan. I finished reading it just before you were born. I sure did enjoy it. When you were born, Harry, so big and strong, I said to everybody you were going to grow up to be the world's champion fighter. Just like John L. Sullivan.'"

The man who became the "Champion's champion" remembered another trip of his youth.

"We went across the Great Divide by prairie schooner, looking for something better than Creede," Dempsey, who by then had made a couple million dollars in and out of the ring, went on. "It was supposed to be a twelve- or fourteen-day trip. It took us two years, the way we went, looking for mining or railroad work for Joe or Johnny or even for my father. I'll never forget the day one of our two horses died while pulling us upgrade.

"My mother became desperately ill. She fainted a lot, was dizzy and in pain a lot. We turned around finally and got her back to Leadville. My father figured that the altitude was responsible for her sickness, so he decided to send her to my oldest sister, Florence, who lived in Denver. Denver!—to cure my mother's altitude sickness!

"There was just enough money to buy a ticket for my mother, but she refused to go without the baby, Bruce, Elsie, and me. So she set off with a ticket for herself, a dollar in change, two ticketless half-fare children, and little Bruce in her arms.

"Pretty soon the conductor came along. He was a mean-looking bastard. He took my mother's ticket, looked at Elsie and me, and demanded our half-fare tickets.

"My mother looked up at him and said, 'I'm very sick.' That's all she said. Then she opened her purse and showed him the pitiful change it contained.

"'Okay,' he said after a while, 'the girl can travel free. But that boy has to have a half-fare ticket or he gets thrown off at the next station.'

"You know, no matter how poor you are you never get used to humiliation. I was humiliated. And terribly frightened that I'd have to leave my mother.

"But then a man across the aisle beckoned to me. I went over. He said, very low, 'I don't think the conductor will bother you, kid. Tell your mother not to worry. I'll pay for you.'

"That ended that. But I'll never forget the impression it made on me. I got a sudden feeling, I guess you'd call it a lust, to be rich like the wonderful fellow across the aisle. Rich, so I would never be humiliated or frightened again. Never.

"My mother and father were Mormon converts. But he was a Jack Mormon, one who doesn't live by the book. He drank, smoked, took coffee, and violated most all the laws of a faith he believed in. He'd grin and say, 'I know the church is right but I'm just too weak to live up to all those rules.'

"My mother was a real Mormon, from the day she got the faith until the day she died in 1943. I think her death told a lot about her life. She was attended in her last days by a Salt Lake City doctor named Pendleton. He was always too cheerful. He kept asking her, 'And do you feel any better now, Sister Dempsey?'

"She could face facts better than anybody I ever knew, my mother could. And one day she had enough of that fellow. She gave him an answer that summed up her whole life. She said, 'Dr. Pendleton, you know very well I'm dying. If you ask me how I feel again I'll get out of this bed and punch you in the nose.'

"He didn't get another chance to inquire about her health. She died . . .

"I loved my mother," the iron-fisted old champ said softly.

There have been courageous mothers who never had children of their own.

Edith Taylor, for one.

This is the story of her love for her husband, Karl. Whether or not he deserved her love, and why he acted the way he did, are questions I can't answer. I'm not going to write about Karl. This story is about his wife.

The story begins in 1950 in the Taylor's small apartment in Waltham, Massachusetts. Edith Taylor was sure that she was, as she often said, "the luckiest woman on our block." She and Karl had been married twenty-three years, and her heart still skipped a beat when he walked into their place at the end of his day's work.

Oh, sure, there'd been tough times over those years, times when Karl had been depressed, unable to keep a job, but she had helped him through the low times and she only loved him more because he needed her. As for Karl, he gave every appearance of a man deeply in love with his wife. On his trips out of town as a United States Government warehouse supervisor, he'd made a point of sending her two or three postcards every day, reporting on where he was, how he was doing, and how he was looking forward to that happy day when he could make a down payment on their home, retire, and they could live together happily the rest of their lives.

In February 1950, the Army sent him to Okinawa to supervise one of its enormous installations. It was going to be a long trip. This time, no little gifts came back to Waltham, but Edith understood. He was putting every cent he saved into the bank for their home-to-be. Hadn't she begged him for years not to spend so much on her, to save it for the house?

The lonesome months dragged on and on. It seemed to Edith that the job over there was taking much longer than either of them had expected. Every time she had reason to believe he'd be coming home, he'd write that he must stay "another three weeks," "another month," "just a couple of months longer."

When Karl had been gone a year, Edith had a happy inspiration. She would buy their home then and there as a surprise for him on the happy day he came back. She was working then in an electronics plant in Waltham, Massachusetts, and saving on every penny earned. It was one of the proudest days of her life when she made the down payment on a cozy, unfinished cottage with lots of trees and a view.

The days sped by because she was busy with her wonderful

surprise. Within two months after the down payment, she earned enough to have the floor laid in the bedroom. The next month, she ordered the insulation. She was getting into debt, she knew, but with what Karl must have saved . . .

She worked feverishly, then desperately, for Karl's letters were coming less often. No gifts she understood. But a few pennies for a postage stamp?

Then, after weeks of silence, came a letter:

"Dear Edith: I wish there were a kinder way to tell you that we are no longer married . . ." it began.

Edith walked to the sofa and sat down. And managed to read the rest of it. Karl's letter told her that he had obtained a Mexican divorce from her by mail in order to marry a Japanese girl named Aiko, the maid-of-all-work assigned to his quarters.

Aiko was nineteen; Edith, forty-eight.

Now, by every familiar scenario, if this were a fictional situation, the rejected wife would first feel shock, then fury. She would fight that quickie paper divorce. She would hate her husband and the strange young wife he had taken. She had been so much in love with him for nearly a quarter of a century! She would seek vengeance for her own shattered life.

But I am describing here what actually did happen. Edith Taylor did not hate Karl. She had loved him so long she was unable to stop loving him. She could picture the situation: a penniless girl, a lonely homesick man who sometimes drank more than he should, constant closeness. Edith somehow made a heroic and successful effort to be proud of her husband. Karl had not done the easy, shameful thing, she decided. He had chosen the hard way of divorce from her, rather than take advantage of the poor young Aiko.

The only thing Edith could not believe was that he had stopped loving her. She made herself accept that he loved Aiko, too. But the difference in their ages, in their backgrounds—this couldn't be the kind of love she and Karl had known! Someday Karl and the Japanese girl would both discover this. Someday, somehow, Karl would come home.

That might take some time, Edith realized. So she sold the little cottage—Karl never knew about it—and wrote him a letter saying that she understood what he had done, she guessed, and please drop her a line from time to time to tell her how he was coming along.

Karl replied. He wrote that he and Aiko were expecting a baby. Marie was born in 1951, and then Helen in 1953. Edith Taylor sent presents to the babies, and Karl's letters increased in number: Helen had a tooth . . . Aiko's English was improving . . . Karl had lost weight. Edith's life now centered on Okinawa, across the world from Waltham. She merely went through the motions of existence in Waltham. Back and forth between her work and her apartment, day and night, her mind was on Karl. Someday he'd come back . . .

But then a terrible letter from him: Karl was dying of lung cancer. Follow-up letters from him were filled with fear, not for himself but for Aiko and his two little girls. He wrote that he had been saving to send them to school in America, but his savings were being wiped out by his cancer treatments. What would become of them?

It was then that Edith Taylor realized that her last gift to Karl could be peace of mind during his final weeks of life. She wrote him that, if Aiko was willing, she would take Marie and Helen and raise them in Waltham.

For many months after Karl's death in Okinawa, Aiko would not let the children go. They were all she had ever known and loved in her life. Yet, she pondered, what could she offer them except the kind of life she herself had had: proverty, servitude, despair. In November 1956, she sent the children to Waltham, addressed to "Dear Aunt Edith."

It was difficult at first for Edith to be a mother, at fifty-four to two little girls who had forgotten the English their father had taught them. But five-year-old Marie and three-year-old Helen learned fast. The fear of strange surroundings left their eyes, their faces grew plump. And Edith, for the first time in years, was hurrying home from work to relieve the baby-sitter and prepare the dinner.

The only sadness in her life by now were the occasional letters from Aiko. In block letters.

"Aunt," one read, "please tell me now what they do. If Marie or Helen cry or not."

It wasn't an easy time for Edith Taylor, keeping things going as aunt-mother-breadwinner. She collapsed one day at the plant and spent the next two weeks in a hospital with pneumonia, first arranging for neighbors to look out for the children.

There, in the new loneliness of her hospital bed, Edith Taylor concluded that she would be old and unable to work before the children were grown. She had thought she had done everything that her love for Karl had asked of her. But now she knew there was one thing more. She must somehow bring the girls' real mother here, too.

She was laughed at when she made application to bring an alien named Mrs. Aiko Azuma Taylor to the United States, all the way from Okinawa. It was then that Edith Taylor wrote me a note, care of the Boston *Record-American,* telling me her story of love and heartbreak and courage beyond the ken of us ordinary mortals. She asked me if I could help her open the door. With the support of the paper and a few good-hearted Joes in Congress, including Jack Javits of New York, a special bill was rushed through, and in August 1957, Aiko Taylor was permitted to enter the United States.

As the plane landed at New York's International Airport, Edith had a moment of fear. What if she should develop an instant hatred for this woman who had taken Karl away from her? How would that affect the children?

The last person off the plane was a girl so thin and small Edith thought at first she was a child. The tiny passenger could not start down the steps. She stood there transfixed after emerging, clutching the railing. And Edith knew that if she herself was afraid of this confrontation, Aiko was close to panic.

She called Aiko's name and the girl rushed down the steps and into Edith's arms. In that brief moment, as they held each other,

Edith breathed a silent prayer, an impossible prayer that things would somehow turn out all right for all of them.

You know something? The prayer was answered.

I called Edith Taylor to ask her for a progress report, early in July 1974. It turned out to be a happy time to call.

"The girls have grown up darling," she said. "Maria's twenty-three now, has just graduated as a registered nurse, and goes to work next month at New England Baptist Hospital—where Teddy Kennedy was when he broke his back in that plane crash. Maria just married a wonderful boy named Vincent Marcantonio.

"Helen's twenty-one and beautiful. She starts her nurse's training in the fall. Aiko has been working for Hewlett-Packard electronics for ten years. She's a marvelous worker. What good pals we are! The girls call her Mommy. And do you know what they call me?"

"No," I said, shook.

"They call me Mother," the first Mrs. Karl Taylor said with quiet pride. "They're so good. I can brag about them because I didn't give them birth."

She paused, as if she had run out of breath. Then she said, "Excuse me for a minute. I'll be back."

When Edith Taylor came back to the phone her voice was strong again.

"Sorry," she said. "I've had a couple of heart attacks lately, and I had to fetch a little nitroglycerin tablet. Now, if you're going to write something about us, don't give *me* the credit. *They* did it, not me. This whole thing has done more for *me* than for anybody else. God took Karl from me, but He was also so wonderfully kind to me.

"He left me a part of Karl."

Chapter 5

Tender-handed stroke a nettle
And it stings you for your pains.
Grasp it like a man of mettle,
And it soft as silk remains.

AARON HILL (1685–1750)

Courage is not necessarily the province of the hairy-chested, nor is difficult decision-making confined to the Solomons. I once knew a boy who was badgered into going deer hunting by some much more robust teen-agers. He "got" his deer, but not as much as the deer "got" him.

Happened on a rich kid's family ranch in Texas on the opening day of that year's deer season. Our boy mumbled some excuse, but it was wiped out immediately by a single question. A kid asked him, "What are you, chicken or something?" There was no way of telling them that he was a kid who stepped over ants.

So he took the offered gun and shells and was jeeped to the lonely shooting position assigned to him. The jeep and the happy hunters would be back for him, late in the day.

When he felt sure the others were out of sight and sound, the boy tried a random shot. He had broken his right shoulder in a water-skiing accident when he was quite young and it had not healed properly. So when he fired his aimless shot this day on the ranch he did not use his shoulder as a brace. Instead, he tucked the stock of his rifle under his arm and fired away.

The rifle recoiled viciously. The telescopic sight rammed his forehead, gashed it and stunned him.

The boy didn't know the way back to the ranch house, and he would have been too ashamed to go there if he knew. So he stayed put. Eventually the bleeding stopped, and the blood dried on his face, coat and shirt. He felt like a fool for being such a square, and in anger he fired at this tree, that rock, until he discovered, to his relief, that he had used all of his shells but one.

Precisely at that moment, a superb eight-point buck broke cover and bounded into the clearing ahead of the boy like something out of a child's picture book. Instinctively, the boy raised his gun to his weak shoulder and fired. His heart pounded with a pride he had never experienced when he saw the deer stagger and plunge to the ground as if struck by invisible lightning.

So this was hunting! He dismissed the sobering reminder that he had taken life from an exquisite creature. A more powerful emotion surged through him. He was a man, at last, a mature judge of life and of death. He had read enough to know that he—who in good conscience couldn't swat a fly—had bagged a prize that many experienced hunters would consider worth a year's effort. Besides, that rotten kid would never again call him chicken!

But then a shocking thing happened to the boy, as it had been happening to the deer.

The deer was not dead.

The boy called out for help, for advice, and heard only his mockingly immature echo. He was alone with his deer.

It drained all the strength out of him to walk to the place where the deer lay writhing, its soft eyes dilated as it tried to struggle upright. The bullet had struck its backbone and cruelly imbedded itself.

Through the surge of compassion and remorse a voice inside the boy now reminded him, with burning insistence, that he must put this gentle inoffensive creature "out of its misery." He searched his pockets in the forlorn hope of finding a bullet he knew would not be there. Again he called out the names of his friends until he was hoarse, but he heard only the gasps of the deer.

The boy picked up a rock bigger than his hand. He knelt next to the deer and, after a time of torment such as he had never known, he began trying to kill the helpless animal. The thump, thump, thump of the rock resounded slower and slower. The boy put the bloody stone aside. He was afraid he was going to become ill. He dropped his face in his hands and wept.

The deer still lived, its agony more apparent than ever. The boy thought briefly of using the empty gun as a bludgeon, but he was incapable of hitting the dying deer even once more. Then, shuddering as with a great fever, he took hold of the antlers and threw his weight across the head until, after an eternity, he felt the neck snap and the deer's last agony subside.

The boy rolled away and lay there panting, eyes shut. The wound on his forehead had reopened and leaked blood down his face to his lips. It didn't matter. He wished to die.

Then, after an eternity, a great commotion. The jeep had returned with its boisterous hunters. None of them had got anything. There were screams of delight when they saw the dead deer, and they pounded the boy's back with their congratulations.

The deer season had opened.

Chapter 6

Laugh, and the world laughs with you;
Weep, and you weep alone;
For the sad old earth must borrow its mirth,
But has trouble enough of its own.
ELLA WHEELER WILCOX (1850–1919)

Nobody was a better audience for Ring Lardner's sportswriting, columns, short stories, and his rarely audible banter than his good friend Grantland Rice, dean of all the deans of American sportswriting.

Lardner could always break up Rice. "Granny" was one of the first to read Lardner's immortal answer to a bothersome child who asked too many questions on the auto trip that liberated the Lardner family from Niles, Michigan, and brought them to New York. The question that broke the elder Lardner's back was: "Daddy, why do the car's wheels turn when we are moving?" Lardner, writing about the agonies of the trip, wrote: " 'Shut up,' father explained."

One of Rice's self-designated chores was to coax Lardner out of his thick reticence. What seemed like the ideal opportunity rose in the early years of the administration of President Harding. Harding, who had owned the ball club at Marion, Ohio, was a great admirer of Lardner's "You know Me Al" series about a bragging Chicago White Sox rookie, written for the *Saturday Evening Post*. The President, hearing that Lardner played a little golf, asked his golfing friend Rice to bring the great humorist to Washington to play a round.

Harding expected to be stricken with laughter throughout the eighteen holes, listening to Lardner's stories. But, except for a half-grunt when he was introduced, Lardner had nothing to say to the President of the United States.

Finally, over a drink at the nineteenth hole, the more-or-less demoralized President said, "Well, Mr. Lardner, it certainly was a pleasure to play with you today."

Lardner just stared at him, funereally.

The President coughed. "Is there anything I can do for you while you're in Washington?" he asked.

"Yes!" Lardner said with a vigor that surprised his host. "Appoint me Ambassador to India."

"India?" Harding repeated incomprehensibly. "I'm not even sure we have diplomatic relations with them. But why India?"

"Because my wife hates Great Neck," Lardner said.

Harding died not too long after that.

In the spring of 1933, when Lardner was dying in a New York hospital, he was turning out a wonderfully adroit piece about radio for *The New Yorker*. (He suggested at the time that a top tune on "The Hit Parade" entitled "Let's Turn Out the Lights and Go to Sleep" become a pornographic record.)

Rice walked in for his daily visit and found him, as usual, sitting up in bed with a large writing pad and pencil on his sheeted lap.

But this day was different.

"Ring!" his old friend said. "You've been crying. What's wrong?"

It took Lardner some time to say it, but he did.

"I've been trying to be funny," he said.

Bugs Baer, peer of Lardner in that pre-TV Golden Age of American humor, when comedians and commentators actually wrote their own stuff, had a more demanding writing schedule than most of them combined. It denied him the luxury of becoming ill. But on one occasion a covey of doctors and friends all but forcibly put him in a hospital for surgery. He insisted on taking along his portable typewriter, on which he beat out his daily article for the Hearst newspapers. Although in pain, no reader suspected that he was other than the happy-go-lucky observer of the human condition who had defined a friend as a person "who can *see* the star in your sapphire," and a recession as a time when "things are so tough hitchhikers will go either way."

Only once during his difficult hospital stay did he tip off his audience, and then barely.

"What kind of Christmas story do you write when you're not sure how much string is left in your ball of twine?" he wrote, and then answered his own question. "You write of hope, goodwill, faith and peace on earth."

Then there was Jim Thurber.

James Grover Thurber was both courageous and outrageous. He made millions laugh at his superb words and weird-o drawings while undergoing the personal tragedy of becoming totally blind. As his last "good" eye neared its full eclipse from glaucoma and cataracts, he tried to write and sometimes sketch his agile thoughts on large sheets of yellow paper, using crayons and searching for what he had accomplished through a huge magnifying glass.

Thurber didn't whimper his way into the blackout of his final years. He roared into it.

"God dammit, why don't you ever talk about my blindness!" he said with sudden fury to one of his best friends, who had taken him to lunch. "Why doesn't *anyone* ever talk to me about it? Everybody knows I'm blind!"

But he could be off-handish about it, too. There was a period as he entered into the last furlong of his vision when he took delight in startling unsuspecting lady dinner partners by wearing a false eye. Nothing too unnerving about that, but Thurber's eye was unique. Its pupil was a tiny American flag, which in good time the dear lady on his left or right would recognize, ventilate a gasp, and sometimes flee.

Thurber's somewhat equally offbeat boss at *The New Yorker*, Harold Ross, concluded on many occasions that Thurber was off his rocker, and vice versa. For example, Thurber once entered a branch of New York's Corn Exchange Bank and Trust Company with an armful of freshly shucked corn and demanded money.

The manager called the police.

Ross had better evidence to support his qualms. Why would Thurber spend so much of his time living in Bermuda and trying to navigate through Bermuda's busy waters in a small sailboat whose prow he had difficulty seeing from his position at the rudder? Why would Thurber let weeks go by when he would send nothing to *The New Yorker,* which was paying him well after a period in his life when he and his wife ate and drank at Tim Costello's saloon in New York City in exchange for drawing its fabled murals? Why would he write and draw for nothing for *The Bermudian* magazine? During his Bermuda years, Thurber did sixty free pieces for *The Bermudian,* including a classic article he illustrated with wonderfully nightmarish characters. It was called "Extinct Animals of Bermuda." Thurber's long-gone species included the Common Thome, the Waffle-Crested Bly, and the Woan—or Larder Fox.

Thurber once settled for a spell in Felicity Hall, a lovely old place in Bermuda where Hervey Allen wrote his memorable *Anthony Adverse.* It was by that time a shrine for visiting Americans. As many as forty tourists a day would rap and enter, while Thurber was trying to work. Two Helen Hokinson types particularly annoyed him.

"This is the place where that book was written?" one lady demanded of Thurber, as if he were the janitor.

"What book?" Jim asked coldly.

The woman turned to her companion and asked, "What did the guide say the name of that book was, Clara?"

Clara threw herself on Thurber's mercy, which that day was largely quicksand. "Don't *you* know what the book's name was?" she pleaded. He ignored her, but just then the first lady, whose name was Myrtle, cried out, "I got it! *Anthony Allen.*"

Thurber sniffed. "Oh, that," he said. "You probably mean the novel by Hervey Adverse. It was nothing."

"How can you say that?" Myrtle said, shocked. "The guide told us it took five years to write."

"That's because he started at the beginning," Thurber said with a frown. "I'm now writing a book I'm calling *Anthony Adverse.* I'm writing it backwards and I expect to finish it in two weeks." The women fled, perhaps fearing assault.

Ross questioned many of Thurber's hilarious cartoons, including the unforgettable one showing a bloblike nude female crouching atop a bookcase while a man, accomplished by a slightly less blobby woman, explains to a nervous visitor he is showing through the place, "That's my wife up there, and this is the *present* Mrs. Harris."

Ross called Thurber at his place in Connecticut.

"Is that woman on the bookcase alive or stuffed, or just dead?" he demanded. Thurber said he would think it over and call back. Which he did.

"She *has* to be alive," he told Ross. "My doctor says a dead woman couldn't support herself on all fours, and my taxidermist says you can't stuff a woman," he explained seriously.

"Then, what the hell's she doing in the house of her former husband with his new wife—naked?" Ross roared.

"You have me there," Thurber replied glacially. "I'm not responsible for the behavior of my characters."

Life was all uphill for Thurber after a brother accidentally shot him in the eye with an arrow at the age of six. The Thurbers in general had a hard time making ends meet. The father was a frustrated politician who never was able to obtain any lucrative office in his native Columbus, Ohio, even though he sported a derby. Jim's mother was a wonderful midwestern Mrs. Malaprop. (Once she admonished her three sons: "Now don't you dare drive all over town without gasoline!")

"Jamie," as Thurber was called around the house, somehow made it to Ohio State University. He was a keen baseball enthusiast and authority, but couldn't go out for the team because of his fading eyes and a physique that reminded one biographer of "an emaciated sheepdog." Neither of these failings impressed his World War I draft board. He was repeatedly ordered to appear for a preinduction examination. He could barely see the big "E" on top of the eye chart, much less the ever-diminishing letters and numbers that followed below.

"Matter of fact," he said one grueling day to a short-tempered army ophthalmologist, *"You're* just a blur to me."

"And you're absolutely *nothing* to me!" the boob retorted, never knowing (nor did Thurber) that shortly after the news of his blindness was announced, years later, ten persons from various points of the earth volunteered to give him one of their eyes.

Thurber dropped out of Ohio State in his senior year, though he had gained some campus renown as editor of the university's humor magazine. He and his college classmate, Althea, moved to Paris where he had wangled a job as a code clerk in the U. S. Embassy. But, restless to write, he quit after a short time and took a series of low-scale newspaper and free-lance jobs in Paris, then went back home to Columbus when the money ran out, and finally landed in New York. Those were particularly hard times—the Tim Costello years, they might have been called. Thurber had a burning ambition to make the pages of an equally ambitious *New Yorker* magazine, a publishing phenomenon of the early nineteen twenties—as bright and as hard up as Thurber himself. He became convinced that only between its covers could he find a home for what he wished to write about the people he knew and the mores of others, real or imagined. His life became a nightmare of writing, rewriting, and rejection slips from Ross or some other *New Yorker* editor.

Althea correctly diagnosed his trouble: he was "worrying" his stories to death. She recommended they set their alarm clock to sound off raucously exactly forty-five minutes after he started tapping out a new story theme with his two-fingered typewriter approach.

The very first story he wrote under this stern discipline was accepted by *The New Yorker.* It and those that followed sporadically were the thrills of his life, but he needed additional money to pay for his basic needs. He sent Ross a few cartoons, and to his absolute consternation they were accepted. His art form was a melding of vaguely troubled dreams and the wall scratchings of a caveman. His tormented figures were gross caricatures hardly suggestive of anything resembling the image of God. They wavered before the viewer's eyes, but the captions Thurber attached usually reached deep into the roots of the human condition, the eternal war of man vs. woman, the foibles, dreams, resignations and crazed whims that afflict mankind. Thurber's dogs and cats suffered similar despair in their brushes with a hostile nature, and their equal-but-separate canine and feline societies.

When Ross broke down and hired Thurber as a regular member of *The New Yorker* staff in 1927, it was with the understanding that Jim would be a cartoonist, not a writer. Thurber objected, though he needed the steady job quite badly. "I'm a writer," he said, offended. "Cartooning is just tossing cards into a hat!"

Ross insisted that Thurber sit in on staff meetings. Thurber was appalled. To keep madness or fatal boredom at arm's length he constantly doodled or wrote aimless rhymes during these sessions. During one of those stifling seances he drew a seal perched on a rock and looking down at two dots. The seal is saying, "Hmmm! Explorers." He took it home with him and wasn't pleased. It didn't look right. So he redrew it. This time, the seal was perched on the headboard of a bed in which lay a Thurber wife and husband. She's angry, he's baffled. She's saying, "All right, have it your way—you heard a seal bark." Of all the countless thousands of inspired and zany cartoons *The New Yorker* has published over the years, the seal on the bedstead is most fondly remembered.

There were countless others that rocked America before Thurber's lights went out. One showed a fencing match in which one fencer has decapitated his rival—whose head has taken off like a football punt.

"Touché!" the victor shouts.

Thurber became embarrassed by his growing success as a cartoonist. He knew that a certain number of *New Yorker* subscribers were offended by his meager mastery of draftsmanship. But he had his champions, too.

Ross one day defended him against the barbs of another *New Yorker* artist who had called Thurber's work "fifth-rate."

"Thurber's not a fifth-rate artist," Ross said indignantly. "He's a third-rate artist."

Another offbeat supporter was E. B. White, the ultimate essayist who shared his *New Yorker* office with Thurber. Together, they had written a successful book titled *Is Sex Necessary?* It was illustrated by Thurber, but he winced at the sight of the drawings and decided he must become better at cartooning. He bought a drawing board, set it up in White's and his office, and began applying himself to the task of improving his skill. Fortunately, White caught him in time.

"Stop!" White commanded. "If you ever become good, you'll be mediocre."

Dorothy Parker once complained, "These are strange people that Thurber has turned loose upon us. All of them have the outer semblance of unbaked cookies; the women are of a dowdiness so overwhelming that it becomes tremendous style." Another critic once beefed, within earshot of playwright Marc Connelly, "Thurber's women have no sex appeal."

"They have for Thurber men," Connelly said stoutly.

The stultifying staff meetings at *The New Yorker* prompted more than doodling. Sometimes Jim scribbled little things, outlines for stories, even poetry peculiarly his own:

> Allen Lewis, Broosky Burton
>   Went to buy himself a curtain.
> Called on Greenberg, Moe and Mintz,
>   Bought a hundred yards of chintz
>   Stamped with owls and all star-spangled
>   Tried to hang it, fell, and strangled.

Bit by bit, as his eyesight dimmed, Thurber moved toward words rather than cartoons. Ross was skeptical at first, but relented when it became abundantly apparent that Thurber would never draw again. He couldn't see. In time, he couldn't write, except through dictation to his second wife, Helen. Helen Wismer edited several small magazines. She, too, was going blind. Thurber called her his Seeing Wife. Whatever, she led him into new realms that did not involve his cartoons. She led him into that which he prized beyond all else, writing. She saw him through a period in his life, filled with writing, which E. B. White described happily as "like a child skipping rope." Such books as *The White Deer,* which he rewrote twenty-five times, and *The Last Flower,* which he wrote after dinner one night. Their reception was good, but he could never agree with the critics that he was a humorist.

"Humorists lead a life of jumpiness and apprehension," he wrote in reply. "In the house of Life they have the feeling that they have never taken off their overcoats."

But one morning when he was going blind, Thurber got up, found his way to his typewriter and started a story Shakespeare might have praised. He took off his "overcoat" and began it with:

> "We're going through." The Commander's voice was like thin ice breaking. He wore his full-dress uniform with the heavily braided cap pulled down rakishly over one cold, grey eye.
> "We can't make it, sir. It's spoiling for a hurricane, if you ask me."
> "I'm not asking you, Lieutenant Berg," said the Commander. "Throw on the power lights: Rev her up to 8,500! We're going through!"
> The pounding of the cylinders increased: ta-pocketa-pocketa-pocketa-pocketa . . .
> "Not so fast! You're driving too fast!" said Mrs. Mitty. "What are you driving so fast for?"
> "Hmmmm?" said Walter Mitty. He looked at his wife, in the seat beside him, with astonishment . . .

Thurber had groped his way to the core of Everyman's psyche, given a local habitation and a name to man's most secret longing—to dream himself into the robes and skills of Superman. The man whose writing had not impressed Ross now was hailed by Ernest Hemingway as "the best writer in America." In Britain, the prestigious medical journal *Lancet* dealt gravely with what it called the "Walter Mitty Syndrome." "Jamie" would never have to paint another saloon wall.

Indeed, he couldn't have done that even if necessary. His eyes were just about gone. Not even the strong magnifying glass and the chartlike pads and varicolored crayons helped any longer. His hunt-and-peck typing technique went out the window. He simply couldn't see the keys. He started dictating his stories and books to his wife Helen. His "Seeing-Eye" Wife read to him and steered his steps through the perpetual night of his last ten years.

His output during the period most men would consider stark tragedy was phenomenal. He wrote *The War Between Men and Women,* which was partly autobiographical and starred Jack Lemmon in the film version. Sam Goldwyn's production of *The Secret Life of Walter Mitty,* with Danny Kaye as Mitty, was so overdone that Thurber's frail hero was drowned in oceans of Technicolor. Thurber wrote an open letter to Mitty, apologizing to him. His *My Life and Welcome to It* became a television series.

Out of him flowed *The Male Animal,* a moving plea for academic freedom which he wrote with his Ohio State confrère Elliott Nugent, a writer, actor, and director of a Broadway hit and a profitable movie. It was largely Thurber, especially a second-act scene in which Nugent, playing the lead, performed, in the estimation of Broadway publicist and observer Richard Maney, "the funniest drunk scene ever written." It was about the truculence of male penguins, leopards and swans.

Asked by a serious young interviewer how the play was conceived, Thurber said, "The idea came to me one day in October 1938, while I was standing on top of a garage. Whether the idea was there and I walked into it, or whether I unconsciously took the idea there, I do not know. The play, as it happens, has nothing to do with garages. This is one of the soundest things about it."

Incredibly, the blind man became an actor near the end of his life. His collected works were combed and turned into a Broadway review, *A Thurber Carnival,* which had a successful run on Broadway. He was the star of a sketch about a frustrated author whose publisher insisted on sending him a flood of books by the firm's successful authors, and to addresses where he had not lived for years. Thurber was transported onto the stage, evenings and matinees, seated in an easy chair lashed to a treadmill. A certain proportion of each audience did not know he was blind; the knowing proportion was wont to stand up and cheer, with tears, when he finished his perfect bit and was treadmilled out.

He was sixty-five at that point and had lived in exterior darkness for a decade.

"Experiments have shown that the blind man in any field can outproduce his colleagues," he said at the time. "Part of this is the necessity that gives you concentration. I can't look out the window and see swaying boughs or flying birds—or pretty girls, alas. But I've done more than I ever did previously." He gave Ross a swatch of that philosophy one day at lunch. Ross picked up a bottle of Worcestershire sauce and, after a bit, put it down with a thump.

"Goddammit," he said to his luncheon companion, "that's the ten thousandth time I've read the label on the Worcestershire bottle."

Thurber sympathized with him. "Harold," he said, "that's because you're handicapped by vision."

Near the end, Thurber was wept, honored and sung.

"He paid as dearly as any man for his life and genius," said his friend Peter deVries, "with pain and privation, exactions of courage, and physical and moral trials that would have killed a dozen ordinary men."

"His mind was unbelievably restless," E. B. White said of him. "His thoughts were a tangle of baseball scores, Civil War tactical problems, Henry James, personal maladjustments, terrier puppies, literary rip-tides, ancient myths and modern apprehensions. Through this jungle stalked the unpredictable ghosts of his relatives in Columbus, Ohio."

"His is a form of humor which is also a way of saying something serious," wrote poet T. S. Eliot. "There is a criticism of life at the bottom of it."

There were sometimes gentle, sometimes acid criticisms of more than just life. He punctured the posturings of amateur wine fanciers, before he was forced to stop cartooning, by drawing a blob sipping a small glass and saying to a companion blob: "It's a naive domestic Burgundy without any breeding, but I think you'll be amused by its presumption." He took dead aim with his typewriter, too, on the gobbledegook of Washington bureaucracy. And politicians. To wit:

"A politician would write to a girl he was in love with like this: 'I regret that I cannot finalize the normalization of our relationship marriage-wise because I am, as yet, unpredeceased by my wife deathwise.'" When a Conservative columnist wrote, during the blight of the Joe McCarthy years, *"The New Yorker* is Red from top to bottom,"* Thurber was selected to reply. He sent the man a note denying the charge, and added, "It isn't even read from cover to cover."

"Thurber had a firm grasp on confusion," his friend Wolcott Gibbs, another *New Yorker* luminary, wrote of him.

In *The Thirteen Clocks,* one of his last and most enchanting fantasies, Thurber has a character he named the Golux giving some advice to the Prince and the Princess.

"Ride close together," the Golux told the beautiful young couple. "Keep warm. Remember laughter. You'll see it even in the blessed isles of Ever After."

Thurber died in the litter of his good literary intentions. He always thought his next book was going to be "the good one." He died surrounded by thirty-seven stories or articles he had begun and put aside. One of them was titled "A Preface to Something. Please Hold." Another was the title of the autobiography he hoped to write someday.

Its title was *Long Time No See.*

Chapter 7

Of all the senseless bombs dropped on England by the Luftwaffe, the most brainless must have been the one whose target turned out to be a moving-picture theater in East Grinstead, July 1, 1943. A Luftwaffe bomber plot, fleeing homeward after an ineffectual daylight raid on London, shook loose a jammed 500-pounder in the hope of outracing his RAF pursuers. It fell through the overcast that covered that corner of Sussex and, by some astronomical odds-against, plunged into the movie house, filled that Saturday afternoon with children attracted by an American Western. Nearly every family in the town of fifteen thousand was touched directly or sympathetically by the deplorable tragedy.

But there was no time for public mourning. The people of East Grinstead had made a remarkable pact, unique in a world at war. They had made a pledge to be cheerful as they went about their daily rounds . . . smile . . . be hospitable. They had made the pact with Archibald McIndoe, the wizard plastic surgeon from New Zealand, who ran the Queen Victoria Cottage Hospital. Mr. McIndoe, as he was formally addressed, rather than "Doctor," as his American visitors generally called him, remade the faces and arms and hands of badly burned RAF men.

There had been trouble at the hospital before the catastrophe at the movie theater. A once-handsome Spitfire pilot had committed suicide. He had looked at himself in a mirror for the first time since extensive surgery and skin grafting. He found his noseless, earless, scorched face, hung with wattles of raw flesh from other parts of his body, too much to bear.

Mr. McIndoe regarded the incident as a serious crisis that might imperil his whole, noble task of rehabilitation. He forthwith ordered all mirrors removed from the hospital. Then he issued an order that all ambulatory patients must obey:

They must stroll, not dart, through the streets of East Grinstead every day as part of their psychological therapy. No man, however ghastly-looking, was excused.

Mr. McIndoe had prepared the people of East Grinstead, normally sheltered from the shock of seeing disfigured persons at short range. They must not stare at the macabre strollers from the hospital. They must not turn away. By all means, they must not become ill. They must make these ghostly young men feel welcome. They must show them that normal people, like the people of East Grinstead, wanted them to come back to a normal life. They must invite them in for a spot of tea, or something stronger if it was available.

Every Saturday night the pretty girls of the town and the young nurses from the hospital would dance with these effigies of youthful heroes who had been seared by engine fires that had belched into their cockpits and grossly changed them into other people.

"Nursey, you'd never know it, but I was a good-looker and the girlies couldn't get enough of me," a faceless and mostly fingerless pilot croaked from behind his plaster mask one day as I walked with her through his ward.

She came over to him and put her hand on what was left of him.

"Don't I know!" she said with a love in her voice one would want to hear the rest of one's life. "That's what the whole lot of you tell me."

Manly chuckles sounded through the ward.

Chapter 8

*With all this, I consider myself the luckiest man on the face of
the earth.*

HENRY LOUIS GEHRIG (1903–1941)

It is still hard to believe that Lou Gehrig was only thirty-eight years
old when he died of a strange and muscle-wasting disease that still
baffles medical science. He was possibly the strongest and certainly
the most durable of the great major-league baseball players, as his
record of 2,130 consecutive games as first baseman of the New York
Yankees will attest.

Another generation of players and fans tends to accept Lou as
one of those comparatively rare physical specimens to whom all
things muscular come naturally—a dimpled demigod endowed
since birth with all the needed skills, instincts, grace and confidence
that add up to stardom. In Lou's case the reverse was often true.
Though he had clearly demonstrated to assorted scouts that he
could hit the ball a mile—as a member of Columbia University's
ball club—the Yankees sent him through what must have seemed to
him a galling apprenticeship with Hartford, the parent company's
Connecticut penal farm. All of Lou's subsequent records are now
preserved in the Baseball Hall of Fame in Cooperstown, New York.
But there is no file there, excepting the late Frank Graham's tender
biography *Lou Gehrig—A Quiet Hero* (Putnam) that properly ex-
amines this great ballplayer's frustrations and doubts—all of which
he overcame, overpowered, more by the strength of his will than his
approximate acre of muscles.

On the long bus rides with the Hartford team Lou had ample
opportunity to wonder whether the dapper brewer who owned the
Yankees, Jake Ruppert, and Ruppert's burly and sometimes hard-

bitten general manager, Ed Barrow, remembered that he was still alive. He experienced doubt, too, as to whether he was good enough to invade the regular lineup on a team of which his hero, Babe Ruth, was an incomparable star.

But a greater mental block to Gehrig as a minor leaguer was Wally Pipp, the regular first baseman for the Yankees—an accomplished fielder, hitter and runner whose springs apparently never would run down.

Gehrig plugged away. Plays, moves, impulses that came to a Babe Ruth (and, alas, Wally Pipp) caused Lou weeks of the manual labor of practice to learn. His discipline would have put a galley slave to shame.

After tantalizing tastes of what it was like to be a Yankee, in the springs of 1923 and 1924, Gehrig was shipped back to Hartford. But Miller Huggins, the Yankee manager, kept tabs on him. He brought Gehrig back to the big team's bench in 1925. In Huggins' opinion, Lou was "ready," perhaps not ready to relieve Pipp of his job—which he had held for fourteen years—but for other things, one of which Lou found degrading: Huggins made him Ruth's baby-sitter.

That job lasted only a short time during spring training in 1925. Gehrig's idea of how to spend an afternoon when a game is rained out was to take in a movie. But he had his orders from Huggins: Don't let the big guy out of your sight. Huggins, who had tried every other method of domesticating the least manageable ballplayer of them all, came up with the demented idea that Gehrig's sobriety, good manners, and Frank Merriwell wholesomeness would change Ruth's lifestyle.

Came a rainy afternoon in Birmingham. The Yankees' train was not due to leave for the next town on the exhibition schedule until 7 P.M. By noon it was abundantly apparent that Babe had no more intention of going to a movie with his clean-living new roommate, and fan, than he had of resigning from the Yankees and taking a job as a steel-mill hand. Prodded by handsome tips, the bellhops of the hotel were already scouring the town for its available booze, beer and ladies of the afternoon.

A good time was had by all in the suite, bye and bye, except by the Great Man's chaste, bowtied roomie. When Lou was not trying to reform the ladies, he entertained dark fears that Babe might succumb to the rigors of the rainy afternoon and that he, Lou, would be blamed for not having properly protected baseball's irreplaceable star. Dusk had fallen, and Babe had threatened to, when it came time to go to the train. Lou helped dress the stricken mammoth, wrapped him in his expensive camel's hair coat, cocked the familiar camel's hair cap over his huge head, and led him to the elevator. The lobby was filled with Ruth fans who had waited—in some cases all day long—for a look at him, or were brandishing autograph books. Gehrig clamped a steel grip on Babe's arm, too reverent of him to let a crowd of idolaters see him stagger or hear him mumble, and swept him through the lobby, out the front door, and managed somehow to ease him into a taxi.

Babe was sick in the cab, but Lou cleaned up and providentially got him aboard the train and into his Pullman room without Huggins' notice. Babe went to sleep immediately, but awakened groggily when Lou tried to extricate him from his coat.

"Who the hell are you?" Babe demanded huskily, trying to focus on Lou. He took a clumsy punch at Lou, for good measure, then fell back asleep—like a baby.

June 1, 1925, was just another lackluster day for Gehrig, still benchbound. The Yankees were losing hopelessly to the Washington Senators, who were to win their second American League pennant in a row that season. Huggins called Gehrig's name and sent him in to pinch-hit for Pee Wee Wanninger, the Yankee shortstop. He was an easy out, and trotted crestfallen back to the anonymous portion of the bench reserved for him and other hopefuls.

But it marked the launching of a baseball record which appears to have the least chance of ever being broken—in this age, when baseball managers are quick to bench regulars whose predecessors were expected to cure themselves of similar ailments with a couple of aspirins. The following afternoon as the Yankees began their leisurely movement from their locker room to their dugout, Gehrig took brief advantage of the empty rubbing table and stretched out. Pipp was going to play another century or two, so what did it matter? He closed his eyes for a moment, but then opened them and sat upright quickly. Huggins was standing beside the rubbing table.

"Are you tired?" the little manager asked sarcastically.

"No, sir," Lou said, blushing.

"Good," Huggins said. "You're playing first base today."

June 2, 1925 . . .

It was as if Huggins had touched a trigger that released all the pent-up tension in a watch spring that had been wound up tight for years. Gehrig got three ringing hits that first day as a Yankee regular, scored a run, handled eight putouts and an assist in the field—and Pipp never returned to the sack.

So swift was Lou's full acceptance as a star that he was promoted to the fourth slot in the Yanks' batting order, the "clean up" post which he handled so magnificently for so many years. Lou's fans sometimes embarrassed him by suggesting that "if Ruth wasn't around," Lou would be hailed as the greatest star in the game and reap greater financial awards. But Lou was not a man of chagrin. He was proud of being a Yankee and, in addition to piling up his record for consecutive games played, he was becoming as feared at the plate as the Babe himself. Good rival pitchers who once deliberately walked the Babe in a tight spot gave up on the practice—because immediately beyond Babe lurked Lou. Everybody remembers Babe's 60 home runs in 1927; not nearly as many remember that Lou that same year hit 47 homers and had a batting average of .373 to Babe's .356.

Frank Graham tells of a day against Philadelphia during the 1932 season when Lou made it clear, even to himself, that he need never again feel inferior to the Babe:

"On June 3, at Shibe Park, Lou performed one of the greatest feats in the long history of baseball. George Earnshaw was pitching for the Athletics, and in the first inning Gehrig hit a home run. Going to bat in the fourth, he hit another. He went up for the third time in the fifth—and hit a third home run.

"Connie Mack thought it was about time Earnshaw retired for

the afternoon. So Connie waved him out and called Bill Mahaffey in from the bullpen. Connie always liked Mahaffey. He thought he was a pretty smart pitcher.

" 'Wait, George,' he said as Earnshaw started for the clubhouse. 'I want you to see how Mahaffey pitches to Gehrig.' When Gehrig stepped up to the plate in the seventh, Mahaffey pitched a high fast ball to him—and Lou hit it out of the park.

" 'I see, Connie,' Earnshaw said. 'May I go now?' "

In 1936, a year after Babe had left the Yankees in a huff for a short career-ending stint with the Boston Braves, Yankee manager Joe McCarthy named Lou captain of the team. The post did not entail a great many responsibilities, but Gehrig was pleased. He dominated the Yankee drive to the team's first pennant and World Series title in four years with a .354 batting average, 49 home runs and 152 runs knocked in. And, as had been the case for a decade, he played in every game.

But somebody happened to Lou at the moment he had his first clear shot at being No. 1 on the No. 1 team in baseball. The somebody was rookie Joe DiMaggio, purchased from the San Francisco Seals of the Pacific Coast League for a piddling twenty-five thousand dollars. Seems he had a bad knee and might not last long enough to pick up his first million. Joe hit 29 home runs that year, had a .329 batting average, ran the bases like Mercury, made catches in center field that stunned friend and foe. Joe was box office. Lou? Well, Lou was good "old" steady Lou. Steady as, well, the Yankee Stadium, "The House that Ruth Built."

The Yanks won easily in 1938, Lou's fifteenth year with the ball team. They went on to demolish the Chicago Cubs in the World Series. But Lou's contribution was modest. During the regular season he hit .295, a highly acceptable figure in today's baseball, but a source of great embarrassment for Gehrig in 1938. It was the first time he had hit under .300 since joining the team. DiMag had beat him in home-run production the year before. Lou played through the Series against the Cubs, but the four hits he got in fourteen times at bat were all singles.

The first hint I had that Lou's problem was more sinister than a routine slump that year was provided by a wild-and-wooly Washington pitcher named Joe Krakauskas. After a game at Yankee Stadium he told Shirley Povich of the Washington *Post* and me that a frightening thing had happened to him while pitching against Gehrig. Joe had uncorked his high inside fast ball with the expectation that Lou would move back and take it, as a ball. Instead, Krakauskas said, Lou—a renowned judge of balls and strikes—moved closer to the plate.

"My pitch went between his wrists," Joe said, still shaken. "Scared the hell outta me. Something's wrong with Gehrig . . ."

Lou's salary was cut three thousand dollars a year before he went South with the Yankees in 1939. There was no beef from him. He had had a bum year, for him, so the cut was deserved. He'd come back. After all, the Babe played twenty-two years without ever taking good care of himself . . .

Joe McCarthy started Gehrig at first base on opening day of the 1939 season, contemptuous of a fan who, a few days before in an exhibition game at Ebbets Field, had bawled, in earshot of both of them, "Hey, Lou, why don't you give yourself up? What do you want McCarthy to do, burn that uniform off you?"

Lou hobbled as far into the 1939 season as May 2. Then, on the morning of the first game of a series against Detroit, he called McCarthy on the hotel's house phone and asked to see him.

"I'm benching myself, Joe," he said, once in the manager's suite. McCarthy did not speak.

"For the good of the team," Lou went on. "I can't tell you how grateful I am to you for the kindness you've shown me, and your patience . . . I just can't seem to get going. The time has come for me to quit."

McCarthy snorted and told him to forget the consecutive-games-played record, take a week or two off, and he'd come back strong.

Gehrig shook his head. "I can't go on, Joe," he said. "Johnny Murphy told me so."

McCarthy cursed the relief pitcher.

"I didn't mean it that way, Joe," Gehrig said. "All the boys have been swell to me. Nobody's said a word that would hurt my feelings. But Johnny said something the other day that made me know it was time for me to get out of the lineup . . . and all he meant to do was to be encouraging."

McCarthy, still angry, asked for details.

"You remember the last play in that last game we played at the Stadium?" Lou asked. "A ball was hit between the box and first base. Johnny fielded it, and I got back to first just in time to take the throw from him."

"So?"

"So, well, I had a hard time getting back there, Joe," Lou said. "I should have been there in plenty of time. I made the put-out, but when Johnny and I were trotting to the bench he said, 'Nice play, Lou.' I knew then it was time to quit. The boys were beginning to feel sorry for me."

At the urging of his devoted wife, Eleanor, Lou checked into the Mayo Clinic in Rochester, Minnesota. In due time he emerged with a bleak "To Whom It May Concern" document signed by the eminent Dr. Harold C. Harbeing:

"This is to certify that Mr. Lou Gehrig has been under examination at the Mayo Clinic from June 13 to June 19, 1939, inclusive. After a careful and complete examination, it was found that he is suffering from amyotrophic lateral sclerosis. This type of illness involves the motor pathways and cells of the central nervous system and, in lay terms, is known as a form of chronic poliomyelitis—infantile paralysis.

"The nature of this trouble makes it such that Mr. Gehrig will be unable to continue his active participation as a baseball player, inasmuch as it is advisable that he conserve his muscular energy. He could, however, continue in some executive capacity."

Lou returned to the team for the remainder of the 1939 season, slowly suiting up each day, taking McCarthy's lineups to home plate to deliver to the umpires before each game. It was his only duty as captain. It was another winning season for the Yankees, but hardly for Lou. The short walk from the dugout to home plate and back exhausted him. But more exhausting was a cruel (but mostly true) story in the New York *Daily News* to the effect that some of his teammates had become afraid of drinking out of the Yankee dugout's drinking fountain after Lou used it.

"Gehrig Appreciation Day" (July 4, 1939) was one of those emotional salutes which only baseball seems able to produce: packed stands, the prospect of a double-header win over the Washington Senators, a peppery speech from Mayor Fiorello LaGuardia, the presence of Yankee fan and Gehrig buff Postmaster General Jim Farley, and the array of rheumatic and fattening old teammates of yesteryear. And The Family in a sidelines box. Presents and trophies filled a table.

For Lou, now beginning to hollow out from his disease, one basic ingredient was missing. Babe Ruth wasn't there. Babe, the one he wanted to be there more than he wanted any of his old buddies, had not answered the invitations or the management's phone calls.

Then, with little warning, a great commotion and rustle and rattle in the stadium. The Babe was entering. He magnetized every eye, activated every tongue. Lou wheezed a prayer of thanksgiving.

The ceremony between games of the double-header was not calculated to be anything requiring a stiff upper lip. Joe McCarthy's voice cracked as he began his prepared tribute. He promptly abandoned his script and blurted, "Don't let's cry about this . . ." which had just the opposite effect among the fans.

When Lou's turn came, he, too, pocketed the small speech he had worked on the night before. He swallowed a few times to make his voice stronger, then haltingly said:

"They say I've had a bad break. But when the office force and the groundkeepers and even the Giants from across the river, whom we'd give our right arm to beat in the World Series—when *they* remember you, that's something . . . and when you have a wonderful father and mother who worked hard to give you an education . . . and a wonderful wife . . ."

His words began to slither when he tried to say something about Jake Ruppert and Miller Huggins, dead, and McCarthy, Barrow and Bill Dickey, alive.

But nobody missed his ending.

"I may have been given a bad break," he concluded, briefly touching his nose as if to discourage a sniff, "but I have an awful lot to live for. With all this, I consider myself the luckiest man on the face of the earth."

Babe, the irrepressible, stepped forward, embraced him and blubbered, an act that turned out to be epidemic.

Gehrig made the trip to Cincinnati that fall to watch his old club clobber the Reds in the World Series. He had a good time, but some of his friends found it a troubling experience being around him. Going out to dinner one night, with Dickey at his side, Lou staggered and was on the brink of plunging down the long flight of marble steps that led from the lobby of the Netherlands Plaza hotel to the street level. Dickey made one of the better catches of his life and saved Lou from a possibly fatal fall.

Then there was a scene on the train that brought the victorious Yanks back to New York. Lou spotted his friend Henry McLemore of the United Press and invited him into his drawing room for a drink. A table had been set up. Lou slowly but surely put ice in the glasses, then reached for the partly filled fifth of Johnnie Walker Black Label. He wrapped a bony hand around the cork and tried to pull it loose. It was not in tightly, but he did not have the strength to loosen it. Henry stopped listening to what Lou was saying about the Series. He was mesmerized by Lou's struggle, and too reverent of the man to offer to help. Finally, Lou raised the bottle to his lips, closed his teeth on the cork, and let his elbows drop to the table. The cork stayed in his teeth. He removed it, poured the drinks, and went on with what he had been saying.

Henry got very drunk that night.

Just before he died on June 2, 1941, Lou called me from his office. Mayor LaGuardia had appointed him to the New York City Parole Board to work with and encourage youthful lawbreakers. Gehrig threw himself into the work with everything he had, or had left. He also kept up a lively interest in research into the disease that had driven him out of baseball.

It was a note about the latter that prompted his phone call.

"I've got some good news for you," he said. "Looks like the boys in the labs might have come up with a real breakthrough. They've got some new serum that they've tried on ten of us who have the same problem. And, you know something? It seems to be working on nine out of the ten. How about that?" He was elated.

I tried not to ask the question, but it came out anyway, after a bit.

"How about *you*, Lou?"

Lou said, "Well, it didn't work on me. But how about that for an average?—nine out of ten! Isn't that great?"

I said yes, it was great.

So was he.

Chapter 9

He [the writer] must teach himself that the basest of all things is to be afraid; and, teaching himself that, forget it forever, leaving no room in his workshop for anything but the old verities and truths of the heart, the old universal truths lacking which any story is ephemeral and doomed—love and honor and pity and pride and compassion and sacrifice.

WILLIAM FAULKNER (1897–1962)
on accepting the Nobel Prize, 1950.

Ralph McGill, one of the most gentle and affable reporters in the history of American journalism, was perhaps the most pilloried practitioner of his time. Readers of his front-page column for the Atlanta *Constitution*—especially such readers as Lester Maddox, Gene Talmadge, Theodore Bilbo, Ku-Kluxers, white-supremacy groups and ignorant rednecks in general—had a ready term for McGill, a man who loved the South as much as or more than he.

They called him a nigger-lover.

When McGill gave up sportswriting in 1938 for more substantial problems affecting the South, there was hardly a handful of black voters in the whole state of Georgia. A black could be arrested or slugged for drinking from a fountain labeled WHITE, using a public toilet restricted to whites, attempting to register his child in a segregated public school, eating at a lunch counter, taking a seat in the front of a bus, or applying for a room in a downtown Atlanta hotel.

When McGill died in 1969, there was a black associate justice on the Supreme Court; a black man in the United States Senate; half a dozen and more blacks in the House of Representatives; and black mayors in Washington, D.C.; Cleveland, Ohio; Newark, New Jersey; and Gary, Indiana. Schools all over the land had been integrated, some after bloodshed and bitter litigation in the courts. His friends mourned his passing for many reasons, one of them being that he didn't live quite long enough to see his young friend,

Maynard Holbrooke Jackson, elected the first black mayor of Atlanta.

McGill took no bows for the remarkable effect his writings had on Atlanta, the state of Georgia, the South, and the nation in general. He was awarded the Pulitzer Prize in 1959 for his crusading over the years. The citation mentioned the righteous wrath in his coverage of the bombing of an integrated school in Clinton, Tennessee, and of an Atlanta synagogue. In the wake of the award, *The Saturday Review* asked him how he felt about the newest and most treasured of his citations as a newspaperman.

"Frustrated," Ralph wrote back. "Frustrated and sad that in a lifetime I've been able to change so little with so many words."

There was none of the professional reformer in the words and manner of Ralph McGill. He drew his sword only when his strong conscience absolutely compelled him to. He wasn't a crusading Westbrook Pegler, who devoted the later years of his life to flogging Eleanor Roosevelt, nor was he one to consign a politician to the gallows like a Drew Pearson or Jack Anderson. Normally, he was not out for scalps, only for a more subtle form of surgery, a change of heart.

I was once sent to Atlanta to do a series on Martin Luther King. It was a troubling assignment because my editors were in disagreement over the hotly controversial figure. Milton Kaplan of our New York office was convinced that Dr. King was an unbeatified saint who would be remembered with Gandhi. David Sentner, our Washington bureau chief who had a good pipeline into J. Edgar Hoover's office, considered the Negro leader an undercover Communist, and had a photo showing him attending what was called a "Communist school." Dave, a fine editor, also produced an unsigned but clearly FBI-written memo expressing Hoover's suspicions about King.

So, upon arriving in Atlanta and before going to the Ebenezer Baptist Church where Pastor King held forth that day at the funeral of a murdered friend, I called Ralph. He took me to lunch at his club. And I told him about my internecine problem. He burst out laughing.

"So what's new?" he said. "I get that kind of division twenty-four hours a day. Particularly right here in this club. You go get your series. You'll find Dr. King a wonderful, brave, patriotic guy. It's his guts that gets him in trouble."

Ralph didn't realize it, apparently, but he was talking about himself.

It was an understatement.

He kept writing what he believed was right and just in the face of odds that would have brought a wail of despair from the prophet Job. His was often a lone voice crying in the wilderness of ancient white supremacy that reached back to the coming of the first slaves to America. Georgia's White Citizens Councils had a nickname for him in their scurrilous press—"Rastus." It was practically a compliment compared to other names he was called by militant defenders of the South's status quo. "Nigger-lovin' Commie son of a bitch" was also relatively mild. He was shot at, at least once, threatened in hate mail too many times to compute. Garbage trucks dumped their reeking refuse on his lawn. Crosses were burned there, too. Robed Ku-Kluxers picketed the offices of the *Constitution*. The newspaper's advertisers were subjected to boycotts. Ralph's home phone would ring in the dead of night and, because he was a reporter to the core, he'd get up and answer it. It might be the office, calling about a breaking story.

But most times it was some fork-tongued anonymous voice, giving vent to fulsome filth. When he was out of town to cover a national convention or make a speech, it was his ailing wife who would answer the phone and take the vilest kind of abuse.

He arranged for an unlisted number many times. But some redneck at the phone company would spread the word, and the calls would continue.

"Those calls hastened Mary Elizabeth's death," he told me after he lost his beloved wife.

Almost any writer with a by-line column that was syndicated through much of the country, and who was as besieged as Ralph McGill was, would have been tempted to use it as a weapon against his foes. But Ralph was slow to anger. He felt that, given enough time and words, he could persuade those who bitterly opposed him to remember that "we're all God's chillun." But at times it must have seemed to him as futile as trying to spoon the Atlantic dry.

He once said that his great failing as a newsman was that he could see both sides of an issue. Thus he was able, in a sense, to forgive or comprehend what the South had done to the Negro. He once wrote that the odds were overwhelming that a black man, treated badly by his boss, would make an effort to understand. ("He knows he's wrong. He knows it's hard to be a nigger. But he can't do anything about it.") But McGill also wrote, "What the black man never knew was how often the white man turned away from the Negro with a heavy heart . . . or how often that man went to the back pantry and poured himself a stiff drink and said, 'Damn the first man to bring slaves here.'"

McGill was inclined to laugh at reports on how Gene Talmadge used to snap his red suspenders during fire-and-brimstone stump speeches denouncing him, and whip his wool-hat audiences to a froth of hatred.

"I can't dislike old Gene personally," McGill wrote in answer to one of the attacks. "And to be honest about it, I've had a try at it."

But for all his sweetness and light, he could also give a pretty good imitation of Christ cleaning out the temple.

He found it hard to be patient at times with the city fathers of Atlanta. Once they voted to construct a horse ring for fifty thousand dollars in an all-white park—at a time when he was campaigning for a park that blacks could use. "This is the height of folly and injustice," he stormed in his column. Two years before the Supreme Court handed down its historic decision on civil rights, McGill wrote a column he called "One of These Days It Will Be Monday." Monday is the day when the High Court's decisions are announced.

When the Warren Court expressed the new law of the land, McGill thought instinctively of his home region: "In all America, no one was so lucky as the Southerner who was part of this social revolution—to reaffirm the principles of what we have called the American dream."

The subsequent disorders at Little Rock, Ole Miss, and elsewhere pained him grievously.

"This is the harvest," he wrote. "It is the harvest of the defiance of the courts and the encouragement of citizens to defy the law. It is the harvest of many southern politicians and so-called Christian ministers who have chosen to preach hate rather than compassion. For a long time now it has been needful for all Americans to stand up and be counted on the side of law, even when to do so goes against personal beliefs and emotions."

Ralph McGill was not a prophet without honor. President Johnson bestowed upon him the nation's highest civilian award, the Medal of Freedom. Harvard, Columbia, Notre Dame and others awarded him honorary doctorates. His book *The South and the Southerner* won wide acclaim. His mail was filled with speaking invitations. He'd go to Upper Volta to speak to a group of youngsters, but drew the line when invited to speak to Atlanta "service" clubs. He'd say he was sorry—"But I could never trust men who get together in the middle of the day and sing songs cold sober." (Perhaps he was remembering a midday as a young reporter, interviewing one of his favorite poets, Edna St. Vincent Millay. Edna was burning her candle at both ends at the time, and asked him if he knew where she could get a drink. Ralph sent a bellhop out for a bottle of bootleg gin, and the two of them killed it.)

He was not without honor in his own home town, either. He treasured one whispered tribute he received while dining at an Atlanta restaurant one night. An old Negro waiter leaned over him and made so bold as to confide: "Thank you for what you write."

McGill loved the South, no matter how much he was castigated there, and no matter how much he chided it to mend its old ways. He loved it, he once said while under heavy bombardment, "like a parent loves a crippled child." He saw beauty in ordinary southern things: the small farm in Tennessee where he was born, the red clay back roads, the smell of burning pine, the laundry hanging out to dry. He reveled when the Happy Day came:

"Voting rights legislation and reapportionment are at work in the dough of Dixie living!" he exulted. "The South is industrializing. It is attracting persons from other regions and educating more of its own people, who do not and will not any longer accept the old racist hatreds and myths."

His great heart stopped beating at what he would have considered a fitting time. He had just finished having dinner, at a formerly restricted club, with a Negro educator.

Ralph's old friend, Bill Howland of *Time* magazine, said it all at the funeral:

"Mac had guts when it took guts to have guts."

Chapter 10

I see God as short, black, and handicapped . . . no arms.
Shirley Price, computer specialist, NASA, Houston

When the six members of the panel, at the annual meeting in Washington, of the President's Committee on Employment of the Handicapped were wheeled to their places on the stage of the hotel auditorium, I, serving as the uneasy moderator, asked a general question:

"What's the toughest thing you've had to do today?"

Bill Passmore of East Chicago, Indiana, whose legs are off up to his hips as a result of a high-school football injury, was first to speak.

"I haven't found things too tough today," the truncated but unconcerned black man said with a voice much stronger than his body. "Things really work out for you if you put all your trust in God. Nothing can be too tough after that. Everything works out just fine." His smile was as honest as he.

A pretty little girl named Judy Taylor, a paraplegic attending Michigan State University, activated the audio equipment that was part of her battery-driven chair and said into Bill's mike: "The toughest thing I had to do today is to be here. I really feel strongly torn. There was a vigil that went on all last night for our people, and there's a march going on right now. I belong with my people, my kindred out there in the streets where I believe it's really happening. I'd like to invite or challenge everybody, at the finish of this panel, to leave this hotel and join the handicapped who struggled through the night . . . I chickened out near the Lincoln Memorial early this morning."

Larry Kirk of Aurora, Colorado, a handsome former athlete whose legs were blown off by a land mine in Vietnam, told about a logistic problem. "The hotel where I'm staying is just two blocks from this one, but it took me two hours to get here," he said in a matter-of-fact tone. "The first cab that came, well, the guy said he couldn't take me, said he couldn't lift the chair. I told him about the hotel's basement entrance and a kind of platform from which I could sidle into his cab and then pull the chair in behind me. 'All you have to do is drive,' I said to him. But he still wouldn't take me and off he went.

"It took some time for the second cab to show up, but it broke down just as it got there. The third cab we called never even showed up. So the janitor pushed me over here." Larry paused, then added completely without rancor, "I think the hardest thing I have to do each day is put up with normal people."

The auditorium rattled with applause and the stamping of crutches and canes. There were broad smiles in one section where the words from the stage were being transmitted by sign language.

Larry hadn't finished.

"Acceptance of your handicap, I think, is basic for all handicapped people," he said earnestly. "Being accepted is the tough thing. I've got to believe that we are starting to move out of the Helen Keller era after a couple of hundred—or thousand—years. In case you don't understand what the 'Helen Keller era' means to me, it means the long, long period when normal people didn't know how to react to handicapped people without embarrassment, so they ignored them, or worse. Way back there, the handicapped child was beaten with a stick or locked in a basement or an attic. But now the handicapped have taken it upon themselves to go out and get educated and get active.

"When I say that, I don't mean . . . well, I know my legs aren't going to grow back. But it's important for us to be able to go places and be totally independent . . . to reach light switches, go out the front door of our own houses without tumbling down steps, and when we get to the corner to be able to go across the street on our own and go into the next block, and go to the store and buy a soda pop or a piece of bubblegum, and come home again on our own. With this new activism, we are going to be known and we are going to be heard.

"Take Washington's new subway that's being built. I understand there is a controversy over whether to put in elevators. The opposition says that there are not enough handicapped people to justify that expense. I don't think it's a matter of numbers. I think it's a matter of what is right. In the final analysis, you'll find that the handicapped are the most persecuted people since the Jews in Germany during World War II . . . just with little things. I saw a guy in the restaurant, a paraplegic, get his wheelchair stuck under the table. Ridiculous, but there he was, trapped, and nobody tried to help him. It's something like that every minute. But we're moving around more and more. We're going to grade schools with normal kids. We're becoming engineers, architects, politicians, newspeople. The normal kids are taking that into consideration, and when we reach that point I think we will have achieved just about everything we are trying to achieve."

One of the panel members was Harold Krentz, the young Harvard- and Oxford-trained attorney who was the inspiration for that moving stage and screen play *Butterflies Are Free*. Harold is blind.

And a swift and sure raconteur.

The hall rang with happy laughter when he described some trouble he and his wife had recently had with their car.

"My wife is sighted and she was driving," he began. "Sometimes we alternate. The way Kit drives, I might as well. She has been in two accidents in the last two months, which wasn't easy because we didn't have a car when she was in her second accident. Anyway, the other night we were heading home to Washington from Rockville, Maryland, in the middle of the night when Kit told me she thought something was wrong with the car. She didn't have to tell me; you could hardly breathe in the smoke that was coming out of the motor.

"'What are we going to *do?*' she asked me. Well, I suggested that we drop back thirty yards and punt. Kit didn't find that very amusing. She said, 'You're the husband, you know. You're supposed to have everything worked out.' So I told her to relax; I'd fix the car.

"Folks, I doubt if you've ever seen anything funnier than a blind mechanic. I went underneath the car. I wouldn't know a gas pump from a you know what. But after a bit I said that the trouble was obvious; there was a hole in the hose. I didn't know where the hose was, or whether we had one, but it sounded logical to me. The next thing was to get a lift. I told her I'd hide in the bushes until she thumbed down a car, and when she did I'd jump out and hop in the car. It worked!"

The young lawyer's brow furrowed, his mood changed, and the audience hushed. He said he would like to comment on a previous speaker's expressed desire to be regarded by the able-bodied as normal.

"I'd like to amend that slightly and say we *are* normal," Krentz said, searching the battered room with sightless eyes. "My ambition, for example, was to become a lawyer. Now I am a lawyer. I am married to a great girl. My ambitions are to make her happy and eventually to make our kids happy when we have them, and to be a top-notch attorney. These are ambitions that are completely normal.

"The people who are handicapped, frankly, are the people who are 'normal.' The so-called 'normal' people who tend not to get as much out of life as they should, but just exist from day to day. Life for them is one big yawn. Whatever abilities I have I must develop to the fullest. Self-pity is a luxury I can't engage in. I must live life to the hilt. If any of you have seen the way I cross streets, you'll know. I wave my cane wildly over my head, repeat all the prayers I know, and run. If I'm going to be hit, I hope it will be by a Rolls-Royce.

"But, seriously, I think that the ones who have real problems to overcome are not us. We have had to fight our battles. If anything, we have developed a certain security, a certain understanding, a certain strength that people in our society should take lessons from. When we say we have something to contribute, I think it's much more than that. I think it's time people started learning from *us*!"

Larry Kirk came back on:

"Many of us here today had their traumatic experiences at birth. I was twenty-eight years, ten months and twenty-eight days old when my legs were blown off in Vietnam. I had been very athletic. I lettered in six sports in my senior year in high school. So I've been on both sides of the fence.

"I've concluded that being handicapped is not a physical condition; it's a mental condition. If what's left of your parts work, but your brain doesn't, then you're handicapped. Everything came easy for me, once upon a time. Everything I ever tried to do, whether it was sports or dancing or just anything, was a breeze. But now life has become challenging to me to the point where I enjoy competing with people, everybody, and I'll compete with you on anything within reason, and enjoy beating you at it. Before, that was just something I took for granted."

I asked a final question: "Do you think God gave you a bad shake?" Three of the panelists chose to field that one.

Bill Passmore said: "I was in the hospital for about five years after I got hurt in football, undergoing amputations and all sorts of things. I never once felt that God was doing me any harm. Instead, I thought that God had done me some good because He made me stop and re-evaluate my life and my goals, and thank Him for what I had left. It's not what you don't have, it's what you do have that means so much. I've taken what God has left me and tried to rally around it and let it become an asset instead of a liability. If each of us in our daily lives will reach out and touch or comfort somebody, it will be a much better world. God has made me feel a much better man."

Kirk was surprised by the question.

"Blame God?" he asked with a grin. "That's a big one. You can't blame anybody. I always figure there has to be a reason for everything that happens to you. If this hadn't happened to me I would've probably gone through life being a professional soldier and an athlete in my spare time, and that would've been that. I've now learned to reach out, as Bill says, and touch people, work with people, become totally immersed in all types of civic action, things I might never have been exposed to. I think God saw a purpose or a need, and so He just used me. Gee, I hope I do a good job."

The blind lawyer took over.

"Okay, we all have to be very honest with ourselves," he said, as if summing up a case before a jury. "At some point one may say to himself, Hey, wait a minute, there is one of three explanations for your condition: One, God is dead; two, God has a warped sense of humor; and three, there's got to be some reason behind this. I had to think this out and fight this out, and I've come foursquare to the conclusion that it's number three.

"God has taken extremely good care of me: Scarsdale High School, Harvard, Oxford. I work for a law firm that seems fairly happy with my work. I'm married to a fantastic girl. I find that as long as I leave things to God, I do fine. Now, this is not to mean that I don't wish that I could see. I wish I could see my wife. I can't. But I have no intention of having somebody put me down in a hole and throw some dead leaves over me. There are an awful lot of defeats that I hope to turn into victories. There's an awful lot I intend to do before I'm done. I'm extremely grateful to God . . . but that doesn't mean we don't have our battles periodically."

"I see God as short, black, and handicapped . . . no arms," said Miss Price, who is short, black, has no hands, is superbly educated and articulate, and tames computers at the Manned Space Center near Houston.

"You just make Him what you make Him, based on whatever life is to you. God is something within you. If all of us were to draw a picture that had not been instilled in our minds from the past by someone else's imagination as to what he saw God as, I guarantee you not one of us would come up with what God looks like.

"All I know is that God and I have battles," continued the beautifully featured girl with the neat Afro. "God always wins. I'm going to give you the story about the first time He won, because I always think about it. On March 9, 1945, my mother was in labor. My father had gone to work. There were seven other kids in our family when it was time for me to make my grand, dramatic entrance. My mother had lost her water in the seventh month, and therefore it was a dry birth. I had to come the hard way, feet first, and that turned out to be God's way of telling me, 'Shirley, your feet will be your hands.'

"When I was born, instead of the doctor spanking me on the hind part to bring life, he was frightened to death. In the first place, I was real black, full of hair, and had no hands. He was petrified. I was about twelve inches long. He immediately wrapped me in a blanket, stuffed me in a shoebox, and put the lid on it.

"When my mother finally came to herself, she asked her neighbor, 'Clarice, what is it?' Clarice said, 'Katherine, it was a beautiful little girl.' My mother said, 'Well, if it was such a beautiful little girl, why is it that I don't hear her hollering? All my kids holler.' Clarice said, 'Well, the doctor said she was born dead. She's dead. Born dead.'

"By that time, fifteen or twenty minutes had passed. The doctor had gone. Clarice started to cry. She said, 'Katherine, the baby wasn't really born dead, but she doesn't have any hands and not much of any arms, so the doctor just didn't try.'

"God didn't give my mother time to think about her condition. She just jumped up and said, 'I don't care if she doesn't have legs, hands, feet, arms, or head. She's *mine,* and I want her.'

"So Clarice lifted the lid off the shoebox, poured a dipper of water on me, and I kicked my way out of that blanket, and I've been kicking ever since."

The assembly of handicapped cheered. When the applause died down, Shirley finished what she had started to say:

"I've had more than that one experience with God, but it's that original experience that makes me so strongly believe there must be a reason why I'm here. I am not going anywhere but up, up, by God up, until I reach it!"

> **cool** (ˈkül) adj 1: moderately
> cold 2: protecting from heat 3:
> not excited: CALM 4: not ardent
> 5: indicating dislike 6: IMPUDENT
> 7 *slang:* very good 8: employing
> understatement *syn* chilly, com-
> posed, collected, unruffled, non-
> chalant.
> Webster's Concise Family Dictionary

F.D.R. was resting in bed at the White House during a particularly difficult period of World War II. A friend dropped by to see him.

"Mr. President," the caller said, "I marvel at the way you bear up under the terrible burdens of this war. Never has a man had to carry more of a burden."

"Oh, I've had worse trouble," Roosevelt said, cocking his cigarette holder at a jaunty angle and beaming.

"That's not possible," the friend said. "The whole Free World is on your back, looking to you to keep it free."

Roosevelt's smile faded a bit as he looked at his friend and said, "Did you ever lie in bed like this and look down your pajama leg to a big toe, concentrate on it and pray and pray and pray, and strain and sweat and curse, and not be able to move it so much as a quarter of an inch? Fail miserably, time after time after time."

The friend stood mute.

The President's smile returned, the cigarette holder resumed its cocky angle.

"That can be a burden, too," he said.

Near the end of his trip to Korea, President-elect Eisenhower was flown in a light plane from the backstretch of the battered Seoul racetrack to a snow-crusted portion of the front where his son John, then a major, was serving. By coincidence or design—which latter device or practice is not unusual during wars when a VIP is in sight —the Navy staged a napalm attack on the forces of North Korea and their allies, "Red" China, as we then preferred to call it. The ground trembled a bit underfoot as Eisenhower lined up for chow with a specially chosen *front-line* group of troops. The group included several South Korean infantrymen who, having filled their trays, were unable to take a bite of the strange fare: pork chops, mashed potatoes, gravy, carrots and peas, deep-dish apple pie and coffee. They turned pale and averted their gaze, clearly yearning for their highly aromatic daily dose of *kim-chee*.

While in line, filling our trays, I asked a tough little GI who looked like a nephew or grandson of Bill Mauldin's Willie or Joe, "You get this kind of grub every day—right?"

"Naw," he said, spearing another pork chop and deluging his mashed potatoes in gravy, "usually they give us steak. What else?"

The GIs who had been selected to sit on Ike's right and left during the luncheon had apparently been picked because of their remarkable ability not to say anything under any circumstance. They didn't even nod during the future President's monologue on how much better the food was in the Korean War than in World War I. They looked like a couple of kids whose nods might be misinterpreted. One was killed in action when sent back to the lines the next day . . . before the picture could be printed in his hometown paper.

Just before we left the site for the return to Seoul, the President-elect took his son aside. None of us in the small group of visitors—in the communications business it is called a "pool"—could hear or tried to hear what transpired between father and son. Ike did most of the talking, judging from the "steam" that came from his lips that cold day. Occasionally John said something too, much less emphatic, as steam goes. At the end of this ectoplasmic dialogue, the impending leader of the Free World, whose presidential campaign pledge had been to end the war in Korea, tapped his son on the arm affectionately, turned briskly, and marched back to his little plane.

A week or so later, I was able to crack through the no-news-today guard that surrounded him while he relaxed and golfed at

Kaneohe Marine Base, Hawaii. We had known each other a little, since I covered the Bonus March on Washington in 1932 when he, then a major, was serving as a smiling buffer for his four-star boss, Army Chief of Staff Douglas MacArthur, who had been given the thankless job of routing out of Washington the thousands of World War I veterans and their families who had gone there seeking an earlier delivery of a promised bonus in the depths of the Great Depression.

So I felt it not particularly out of order, as we had coffee in his Kaneohe cottage, to ask, "General, it's none of my business, but what were you telling Major John that day we went up to the front . . . when you took him aside?"

Eisenhower seemed almost pleased that someone had finally asked him the question.

"I'll tell you what I said to John," he said, "I said, 'John, if you get killed in this war it'll be a terrible thing for your mother and for me, but that's a soldier's life. We take that risk when we put on the uniform. Somehow, your mother and I could live through a thing like that.

"'But for God's sake don't get captured. Don't let them capture you. If you should be captured and they held you over my head, I wouldn't be able to serve as President of the United States.'"

I don't recall exactly what was said after Eisenhower's extraordinarily frank revelation of what he had told his son. My mind was filled with an earlier scene, one that suddenly dovetailed with the present experience, and made grim sense. I recalled a smoky autumn night at the home of a mutual friend, financier and art collector Howard Young, at Ridgefield, Connecticut. Eisenhower, then President of Columbia University, was a weekend guest. Young was kind enough to invite Frank Farrell, the New York columnist, and me to share that weekend with him.

Late on a Saturday night we sat around a fireplace with a scotch. There had been a piece in the *Reader's Digest* about that time about a German plot to capture Eisenhower during World War II. He had been saved from that ultimate personal humiliation, and the Allies had been spared a grievous blow, because Ike's driver had inadvertently avoided an ambush by making a wrong turn on a trip to the front.

Ike scoffed. "There was never a chance that I could be taken prisoner," he said, quite indignantly.

"But why not?" I asked.

He looked at me steadily and then said, very quietly and offhandedly, "I always had a gun."

Which he was saying, in another war and another land, to John.

Wilson Mizner was born in the Yukon, which may have accounted for his cool. He first surfaced as a crushing wit and man of few words when he followed his older brother, Addison, to New York. Addison became one of America's foremost architects, strongly influenced by his studies at the University of Salamanca in Spain; Wilson became a kind of de-horned Devil. As manager of New York's once-discreet Hotel Rand, Wilson introduced such signs in the ornate bar (designed by his brother) as "Carry Out Your Own Dead." He was also the originator of "Be sure it's light, then go to bed." And "A sucker is born every minute, and two to take him."

He was deeply irreligious. Once, in need of fresh money, he stole an early and valuable copy of Da Vinci's "Last Supper" from the salon of the rich widow who had been daffy enough to marry him. He rushed the painting to a "fence" he knew. The thief began giving him an argument over what he would pay for the property. That bored Wilson. "Gimme ten dollars a plate and it's yours," he said.

Wilson enjoyed cocaine. "Snow," he and other addicts called it. Once, while playing in a floating poker game in New York a kibitzer announced, "It's snowing outside."

"Good," Wilson said, without looking up from his cards. "Open the window and hang out my nose."

Mizner had a short but arresting career as manager of Stanley Ketchel, the great but highly unpredictable middleweight champion. Several days before a fight that meant much to them financially, Ketchel disappeared from his training camp and Mizner went searching for him. He found him on the eve of the fight . . . in bed with two girls in a San Francisco opium den. The three were dazed.

"My God, what did you do?" a friend asked Mizner.

Wilson shrugged. "What was there to do?" he asked. "I ordered a pipe and crawled in."

If there was anything that Wilson Mizner had reverence for in life it was the guts of Stanley Ketchel, who once had flattened the monumental Jack Johnson before being flattened in return. On the brink of still another fight, while Mizner was rocking in a chair on the porch of a bungalow he shared with his man, an out-of-breath messenger of doom arrived with terrible news: Ketchel had just been shot dead while making love to the wife of an irate husband who came home at an inconvenient time in the afternoon.

"He's dead . . . dead!" the man cried.

Mizner never stopped rocking.

"Somebody start counting ten over Stanley and he'll get up," he said.

Incredibly, the time came for Wilson Mizner to die, too. Emerging briefly from his coma in a Hollywood hospital in the spring of 1933 (he had been writing movie scripts for good money, but described his experience as "a trip through a sewer in a glass-bottom boat), he noticed that a solicitous young priest was standing at his bedside.

"Hi," Mizner said, "I've just been talking to your boss."

Jackie Gleason was fortunate enough to engage Archbishop Fulton J. Sheen on his TV variety show. The distinguished churchman, whose words of wisdom had vanquished Milton Berle's vulgarities several years before, when they were opposite each other on rival tubes, was communing with himself backstage—as to what he would say on such subjects as faith, hope and charity—when Gleason interrupted his reverie with a loud remark. With the grace of a wounded rhinoceros, Jackie said to him, "Well, Bishop, I see you're looking at the June Taylor dancers as they get ready to go on—right?"—which broke up backstage.

"Yes," Sheen said, guillotining the suggestion. "Even a man on a strict diet has a right to look at the menu."

It was the night before the invasion of a Japanese-held island whose capture would cost an unknown number of American lives. Terribly solemn: lights out on the troopship, chaplain's voice and prayers for the troops' welfare muted.

Then, in the terrible vacuum that followed, the awful black night and the thought of a possibly gruesome dawn, a voice. Nobody to this day knows whose voice it was. But those who were there remember what the voice said.

The voice said: "Anybody want to buy a good watch?"

Other odd things happen under great stress and, in their way, lessen stress.

Former heavyweight champion Jack Sharkey, who had unexpectedly lost his title to mob-controlled Primo Carnera, and the fabled Yankee pitcher Lefty Gomez were caught one night in a German raid while working in a USO show in Italy. All hands were ordered to hit the slit trenches on the double. Sharkey dove into the nearest of them headfirst, a dry belly-flopper. Gomez, equally swift, landed on top of him, a split second later. They lay in that position as the racket of the bombardment continued. It was intolerable.

"We're going to die in this rotten hole in a place I can't even pronounce," Sharkey mourned in the dirt that pressed against his face. "We're going to die!"

"You think so?" Gomez, a wonderfully fey soul, said, his lips close to the former heavyweight-champion-of-the-world's ear.

"I know!" Sharkey shouted angrily above the roar of bombs.

"If that's so," Lefty said, "may I ask you a sports question?"

"Holy Christ," Sharkey said. "What a time for a sports question! What is it?"

"Did you go in the tank for Carnera?" Lefty asked.

How does the greatest heavyweight champion of them all—we're thinking of Jack Dempsey—explain losing his title? Especially to his wife?

Dempsey had that terrible problem the night he returned to his hotel in Philadelphia after losing to Gene Tunney . . . losing his multimillion-dollar championship to underdog Gene Tunney. Dempsey's wife at the time, film star Estelle Taylor, was waiting for him in tears.

"What happened, Gizberg?" she said tearfully, using her pet name for one of the toughest fistfighters who ever lived.

Jack could have offered her half a dozen reasons: he had been out of action for three long years; he had had difficulties with his manager Jack Kearns, other suits and other problems. But he disdained such alibis.

"Honey," he said, "I guess I forgot to duck."

Chapter 12

If you want peace, the thing you've got to du
Is jes' to show you're up to fightin', tu
JAMES RUSSELL LOWELL (1819–1891)

As a kid in a Chicago ghetto, Barney Ross ran errands for a mobster who would have scared Marlon Brando out of *The God-father*—Al Capone. Thus, he could have been rubbed out at a tender age. But Barney lived to become the lightweight and welterweight champion of the world, won a Silver Star as a U. S. Marine in World War II, and conquered the toughest of his rugged foes, narcotics. He, whose square name was Barnet Rasofsky, was the kind of Jew who could play "Adeste Fidelis" on a leaky organ during a Christmas Eve bombardment of Guadalcanal, and know the Latin. Barney was the gentlest of all the fighters I ever covered. His father died when Barney was fourteen. The elder Rasofsky, a Talmudic scholar whose pathetic little grocery store barely supported the parents and their six children, was shot and killed in a holdup that yielded the murderers only pennies, nickels and dimes. He had journeyed all the way from Russia to Chicago to escape the persecutions of the Czar.

The tragedy broke up the family. The widow suffered a nervous breakdown. Neighbors arranged to send the three youngest children to an orphange. Barney and the remaining two children were placed with equally poor relatives.

With no parental restraints, Barney became a school dropout and a product of the environment. Miraculously, he remained clean in the midst of corruption that spanned the spectrum of violence. His sometime patron, Capone, became Public Enemy No. 1, absolute emperor of an army of crooked public officials, police and plug-uglies. There was ample evidence that on one occasion the Capone mob, operating under a flag of truce, gave a testimonial dinner to the leader of a rival mob. After flattering the competitive goon with a series of toasts, tributes and pledges of eternal brotherhood, the Capone people beat him to death on the speaker's platform with a baseball bat.

Barney, a hungry veteran of a thousand street fights while still in his teens, found regular employment in the only profession he knew —outside of running errands. He turned amateur boxer, appearing in matches wherever he could find a tournament, including those conducted by the Catholic Youth Organization. He dropped Rasofsky for "Ross," and Barnet for "Barney." His main reason for changing his name was to conceal from his mother, by then living with relatives, that he was fighting for a living. He feared it might provoke another breakdown. As for making a living as an amateur, he had discovered an ancient practice of amateur athletics, notably in boxing. He hocked his amateur prizes—watches, medals, loving cups, and plaques—and gave the money to his mother.

Barney advanced so rapidly in amateur boxing that there was no way to keep the news from his mother. Knowing neighbors told her, with mounting enthusiasm. So Barney put his arms around her and told her what had been in his mind and heart for some time. He was going to turn professional and make enough money to unite the scattered family in a home of their own. Shortly thereafter, two good Chicago managers, Sammy Pian and Art Winch, took Barney under their wings—for the customarily preposterous percentage—and threw him to the lions of the period: Bat Battalino, Billy Petrolle, and one of the roughest, toughest lightweights of them all, Tony Canzoneri.

In June 1933, three weeks before he toppled Canzoneri as lightweight king, Barney was able to reunite all the Rasofskys in a comfortable Chicago apartment on which he had paid the rent for a year in advance. But an even greater drain on what was left of his hard-won purses was to moochers, down-and-outers, old friends from the ghetto days, and anybody else who came along with a hard-luck tale. There was also the financial wear and tear of living it up. He was by now being ushered to the best tables in the best restaurants and nightclubs and giving the biggest tips. Friends worried about him. One day after he had lost eighteen thousand dollars in the course of a short afternoon at Arlington Park (Chicago) racetrack, good friend Dr. John O'Connell said to him: "Barney, if you had a million dollars in the morning, you wouldn't have a dime left by the time you sat down to dinner." It was an understatement.

But Barney didn't care. He was winning in the ring. Life was beautiful. When he returned to Chicago after beating Jimmy McLarnin for the welterweight title—the first of three fifteen-rounders against McLarnin that are still spoken of with awe in the fight game—Ross was met by a mob of thirty thousand at the train station. A big band played "Chicago." Everybody wanted to touch the hem of his garment, including President Roosevelt, who soon invited him to the White House, addressed him as "Champ," and solicited his aid for the March of Dimes. It never occurred to Barney that this euphoria would end.

It did not end abruptly. Indeed, he and his millions of admirers (and a somewhat lesser number of hangers-on) exulted in his victory over McLarnin in their "rubber" fifteen-rounder, Jimmy having won the second of those classic bouts. The tie-breaker was so close, McLarnin did a happy somersault in his corner while the referee and the judges were adding up their verdicts in favor of Ross.

But thereafter it was largely downhill for Barney. Ceferino Garcia, on his way to the middleweight title, flattened him with his "bolo" punch. Barney got up, as ever, but has no memory of how he survived the last five rounds of his losing fight. It was even worse to behold the night of May 31, 1938, when his welterweight crown was knocked off his bloody head by Henry Armstrong. Barney gallantly held his own against that human buzz saw for the first six rounds, but then began running out of steam. By the end of the tenth, Armstrong had turned Barney's face into a disaster area. He was out on his feet, but not off them. At the end of the eleventh round he could barely lift his arms.

Arthur Donovan, the referee, walked over to the stool where Ross was being given cold towels, smelling salts, and a wound-closing solution called Monsell's.

"I'm sorry, Champ, I've got to stop it," Donovan said to him with the odd tenderness that the fight game somehow can muster.

"No," Barney pleaded. "No, please, Arthur. Let me finish. This is the last favor I'll ever ask of you."

Armstrong, a deeply religious man, "carried" Barney the rest of the way, sometimes clinching with him to hold him up. Barney went the full fifteen. Whether he heard it or not, he was given the greatest ovation, probably, ever tendered a loser.

"Why didn't you quit?" an unfeeling boxing writer asked him in the dressing room after the fight. "You could've been killed."

For Barney it was an odd question. He looked at the writer through the slit in a puffed eye and said, very earnestly, "I won that title in the ring: so why not lose it there?"

Ross opened a cocktail lounge in Chicago after his fighting days and took a second wife—a beautiful young dancer named Cathy. His bistro was well-attended, but mostly by free-loaders, friends (and sometimes complete strangers) in need of money, and jackal bookies salivating over Barney's ever-diminishing horse-playing roll. On one occasion during that dip in his fortunes he heard that his good friend Toots Shor, the New York tavernkeeper, was suffering a periodic depression. Barney packed a bag and flew immediately to New York. He found Toots at the bar.

"Here, Righthand," he said affectionately, using a nickname he and other great pros had given to Toots after hearing Toots's stories about how many muggs he had allegedly flattened with a single punch during his bouncer days. "Here's eight big ones."

Barney flew home broke, having given Toots all he had to his name: eight thousand dollars.

Ross was thirty-three when the Japanese threw their Sunday punch against Pearl Harbor. It took all of his inherent charisma to talk the United States Marine Corps into accepting him and sending him into combat.

The USMC overdid the latter. In a relatively short time, Barney was in a hand-dug ditch guarding what was left of Henderson Field on Guadalcanal, shooting a gun to protect dead and wounded buddies through nightmarish Japanese attacks by land and sea. He was wounded several times and came down with malaria. He needed help, as he did the night he fought Armstrong.

It came on time: the wisdom and kindness of a Vincentian chaplain, Fr. Frederick Gehring, and several Navy corpsmen.

The Catholic missionary later wrote a moving story about his Jewish friend Barney for the *Reader's Digest*.

The Navy corpsmen, unable to listen to their boyhood hero scream with pain, shot Barney full of morphine. It eased the temporary pain, but turned him into an addict.

When he was able to navigate, the Marines sent their by now gray-haired ex-champion of the world back to the States to hustle War Bonds from profit-making corporations that had qualms of conscience, sports groups whose treasuries he had added to during his years in the ring, and Rosie the Riveter. He found himself dividing his time between War Bonds pitches and finding doctors who would risk giving him the stuff his every cell now craved.

His old pals, Shor and an equally brave guy named Johnny Broderick, the toughest New York cop of them all, tried unsuccessfully to talk to him about his habit. Barney was not only on the junk but he was also drinking, probably the most lethal combinations of indulgences or needs known to mortal man. In addition, Barney was drinking straight gin on the rocks. Doubles, of course.

"Get off the gin and go back to the old-time hard stuff," he was advised by one of his top admirers, New York public relations man Curly Harris. "Gin will kill you."

What with one thing and another, Barney had to learn from an item in a Broadway columnist's piece that Cathy was divorcing him. That did it. He walked into the office of the great New York District Attorney Frank Hogan, who had never missed one of Barney's fights in the Garden.

"I'm a dope addict, Mr. Hogan," he said, not even sparing himself the benefit of not using the word "addict." Then he added, "Please send me away to someplace that might cure me."

Only a handful of his friends knew that Barney was an addict at the time. But there he was, in effect asking one of the all-time prosecutors to announce it to the nation.

Barney had one other request.

"Can I turn myself in on Monday?" he asked. (It was a Friday when he confronted Hogan.) "And would you please arrange for me to have enough of the stuff to last me over the weekend. I want to go to Grossinger's, where I trained for so many fights. I want to say good-bye to Jennie Grossinger and all the others."

Hogan nodded.

Barney's recession or withdrawal period at the Federal Hospital for narcotics users in Lexington, Kentucky must have been, in its early stages, a scene out of London's Bedlam or Dante's Inferno. He flattened a male nurse who was in charge of doling out his shots. He tried to kill himself by plunging against his cell walls, headfirst.

But the man who had gone through so many agonies in his life—from Chicago to Guadalcanal—tipped the monkey off his back. He kicked the narcotics habit in half the time it took the gamest of his fellow addicts to claw themselves out of hell.

One of the first things he did when he was released was to ask Fr. Gehring (who had frequently visited him in Lexington) to forgive him. "You must've been ashamed of your old Guadalcanal organ player," Barney said. For penance, he sent flowers to the priest's mother on her birthday, enclosing a card that read, "From your boy, Barney."

Barney's great heart bled for the young addicts he worked with after he beat his own problem. He became a crusader, a stern one. Once, in the presence of Fr. Gehring, he roughly lectured a pathetic young man who had come to him and pleaded to be "cured." He spared the kid nothing, gave him both barrels, and in the course of his diatribe Ross did not neglect himself and the degradation he had brought upon himself before his ironclad redemption. The priest was surprised by Barney's tone.

"Why were you so hard on that boy—and yourself?" he asked.

Barney had a quick, firm answer. "Once you become an addict you become a con man," he said, biting off each word. "The addict will give you all kinds of tearful excuses and glib promises. Only an ex-junkie understands this, and he's the only person the addict can't fool." The boy kicked the habit and joined Ross in a crusade to set up proper rehabilitation centers staffed entirely by former addicts.

Barney was prepared to devote the rest of his life to a war against drugs. Cathy was back at his side by then, immensely proud of him, helpful and understanding. This meant so much to Barney. Each day and night he would touch the medallions he wore around his neck—a mezuzah his mother had given him, a Miraculous Medal Gehring had pressed on him during the delirium of his torment.

But one day, after a routine physical checkup, the diagnostician coughed and told Barney the news: after all he had experienced and overcome in life, he now had an enemy he couldn't lick—cancer.

With a little money that had been raised for him by fight promoters and friends, Barney and Cathy moved back to Chicago from New York, where he had had a modest retainer from publicist Milton Blackstone. Barney entered a hospital for cobalt treatments; Cathy moved into a small apartment nearby. He continued his efforts to persuade legislators in several states to take a realistic and more humanistic view of drug addicts and provide proper treatment for them, rather than prison terms. He was able to pay off some of the people he had borrowed from years before, even pushers who had fallen on hard times.

He even pulled himself together long enough to fly to Dallas as a character witness at the 1964 trial of Jack Ruby, murderer of the murderer of John Fitzgerald Kennedy—Lee Harvey Oswald.

That was the last time I talked to my friend Barnet Rasofsky. I was covering the trial.

"Why would you come all this way to say a kind word for a bum like Ruby?" I asked him.

Barney shrugged.

"He used to carry the bucket for me when I was first starting," Barney said. "Later, I never had a chance to say thanks . . . until today."

Chapter 13

You cannot fly like an eagle with the wings of a wren.
WILLIAM HENRY HUDSON (1841–1922)

This, then, is about three eagles . . . Not a wren in the lot.

It became apparent in the nineteen twenties that aviation could never gain substantial standing in the field of transportation unless pilots learned to fly safely in all kinds of weather and at night as well as by day. Fly "blind," that is.

Looking back, it now seems almost inevitable that the man chosen to prove it could be done would be Jimmy Doolittle. If Doolittle had been old enough he would have been famous as the first human being to eat an oyster. If (somewhat later) he had been young enough he would have the first astronaut on the moon.

He hadn't missed much in between those two adventures. The scrappy little airman was the broncobuster of some of the most maverick flying machines that ever took shape from a warped blueprint. It was said of him that it was a waste of money for the designer of a new plane to build it; Jimmy could fly the blueprint. He was the first pilot to cross the United States in less than twenty-four hours, first to complete it in half that time, first to perform an *outside* loop, holder of speed records in Schneider Cup seaplanes against the best competition Europe could offer, and in such all-but-uncontrollable land planes as the highly lethal Gee-Bee, which ended its life spectacularly. The fabric of its stubby wing peeled off during one of Jimmy's very-low-level speed runs. He dived out and set another record (unofficial): safe parachute jump from ground zero.

Jimmy could pick a handkerchief off a runway with a fishhook tacked to the tip of the wing of a Curtiss Hawk, a fighter plane the U.S. was trying to sell to other governments just as we now try to sell infinitely more costly jets abroad—in competition with the French, Russians, British and Swedish. But in those days Doolittle could be depended upon to outdare the opposition, personally. The evening before his announced intention of flying his Hawk across the Andes—it had never been done before in a single-engine plane —he decided it might be fun to try to do a handstand on the window ledge at a hotel cocktail party. He fell out the window, but with the agility of a cat—he had once been a good lightweight boxer—he twisted in midair and landed on his feet instead of his head.

He broke both ankles. The next day he became the first man to fly solo over the Andes. He had ordered his plaster-cast ankles strapped to the floor controls. If his engine had conked . . . well, Doolittle's attitude toward it was that it wouldn't have *dared*.

But he was much more than a stunt man. He was a first-class instructor with the U. S. Army Air Corps, and the first man to be graduated from the Massachusetts Institute of Technology as a doctor of science in aeronautical engineering.

In 1928, Doolittle was given a leave of absence by the Army to join the Daniel Guggenheim Fund for the Promotion of Aeronautics. He was placed in charge of the Fund's Full Flight Laboratory at Mitchell Field on Long Island. He worked closely with the legendary Elmer Ambrose Sperry, the gyroscope wizard, and Sperry's equally brilliant son. The challenge: how to fly an airplane without seeing where you are going. The moment of truth came on September 24, 1929. Doolittle later described it laconically in a paper published by the Smithsonian Institution:

"We were there and the fog was there . . . The hood over my cockpit was closed. I taxied the plane out and turned into the takeoff direction on the radio beam, took off and flew west in a gradual climb. At about 1,000 feet the airplane was leveled off and a 180-degree turn was made to the left. This course was flown several miles and then another 180 to the left was made. The airplane was lined up on the left of the radio range and a gradual descent started. I leveled off at 200 feet and flew at this altitude until the fan beacon on the east side of the field was passed. From this point the airplane was flown into the ground, using the instrument-landing procedure previously developed.

"This entire flight was made under the hood in a completely covered cockpit which had been carefully sealed to keep out all light. The flight, from takeoff to landing, lasted 15 minutes. It was the first time an airplane had taken off, flown over a set course, and landed by instruments alone."

Doolittle never got around to mentioning then or later that it was also the beginning of a multibillion-dollar industry without which the nations of the world today could not function.

Captain Eddie Rickenbacker, as he preferred to be addressed long after he earned his Air Force Reserve rank of general, lived more lives than the Bengal Lancer. He was one of America's leading racing-car drivers at twenty, the country's ace of aces in World War I at twenty-seven, a busted automobile tycoon at thirty-two, and as he advanced through his middle years, immersed in the charisma of a knight, creator and tough operator of one of the country's top airlines, president of Indianapolis Speedway, financier and —without fail—bon vivant. He was handsomer than Clark Gable, braver than Errol Flynn, and he almost never got around to wearing the insignia of his World War I decorations—France's Croix de Guerre with four palms and its Legion of Honor, his own country's Distinguished Service Cross with *nine* oak-leaf clusters, and the ultimate decoration this country can bestow for courage beyond the call of duty, the Medal of Honor.

Eddie once estimated for his friend Lowell Thomas, who was understandably curious, that he had faced and overcome some one hundred and thirty-five life-or-death situations. Two may suffice to make his point:

On the dismal night of February 27, 1941, one of his Eastern Airlines DC-3s, on which he was a passenger, crashed near Atlanta and scattered its dead and wounded over a gasoline-soaked field whipped by a freezing rain. Eddie, pinned down by the corpse of a steward with whom he had just previously been having a pleasant chat as the plane neared Atlanta, suffered a crushed pelvis, broken leg, and several ribs so badly sundered their jagged ends protruded from his side. One eyeball had popped out on his cheek.

Naturally, he took command—though unable to move.

For hours on end, as rescuers sought the wreckage, Rick husked orders to the wounded not to light cigarettes. The area was shimmering with the fumes of spilled gas. When aid finally arrived at dawn and he was being carried out of the debris, Eddie heard an intern say, "He's more dead than alive. Let's save the live ones."

Rick told him to go to hell.

Two months later, Captain Eddie made an unusual "appearance" in New York while still immobilized in an Atlanta hospital bed. A photographic trick made it possible. It had been his custom since taking charge of the Indianapolis 500 to give a pre-race party for New York sportswriters at Dinty Moore's restaurant. The feature of these occasions was Rick's after-dinner speech, usually a good-natured and profane mock-tirade against three close friends who were in charge of publicizing the race—Steve Hannagan, Joe Copps and Larry Smits. Now, as the 1941 race approached, he sent word to the trio to invite the usual crowd of writers and that he would be there. (At the time he was still in traction and being held together largely by plaster of Paris.)

Then he ordered a platform built over his hospital bed, strong enough to support a sound camera, and the cameraman was instructed to pinpoint his focus only on Rick's face as the battered man looked up from his pillow. When all was in readiness, Rick launched into a salty diatribe against Messrs. Hannagan, Copps and Smits. They, in turn, had followed his instructions and arranged for a life-sized enlargement of Rick in a business suit, mounted on cardboard, with his facial features replaced by a white screen that conformed to the exact shape of his head.

And so on that spooky night at Moore's, the effigy was propped up at Eddie's customary place at the head table after the lights were dimmed, Hannagan introduced "him" as of old, the projectionist found his target, the face, and Rick's manly voice filled the room, giving hell to his chums and directing his filmed gaze or glare at them individually as he called them by name. They had pre-positioned themselves in the room.

Captain Eddie was indestructible, we all agreed, as his talk ended and the lights were turned back on.

Rick confirmed that estimate the following year. In the autumn of 1942—Eddie was fifty-one at the time—he happily accepted an assignment from his friend General "Hap" Arnold, chief of the Army Air Force, to be flown in a B-17 to Melbourne, Australia, to deliver an "eyes only" message to General Douglas MacArthur from Secretary of War Henry Stimson. Wearing his familiar civilian gear, a slightly rumpled business suit and a gray fedora that looked as if it had been slept in, Rick headed out over the Pacific in the four-engine bomber with a customary military crew to which had been added a personal aide, Colonel Hans Christian Adamson, and a GI en route back to Australia after sick leave.

The navigator missed Canton, the tiny island refueling stop in the South Pacific.

The epic of survival that followed after the bomber ran out of fuel and ditched will always remain at least a footnote to man's will to live and overcome against the beady state of appalling odds.

The B-17 sank so swiftly after the rocky ditching that none of those who scrambled out of its escape hatches, dragging the three rubber life rafts, thought to take along with them the water and rations they were soon to need so desperately.

Rick instinctively took charge of the pathetic flotilla, bobbing on an endless sea, totally without communications, helplessly lost. He gave himself the toughest jobs, such as carving into absolutely equal sections the four salvaged oranges that enabled the men to survive the first eight days at sea. He supervised the consumption of the first poor yield of water from a passing rain shower—counting the action of Adam's apples to challenge any man who sipped more than his terribly inadequate share. He was the one who read aloud from the pocket Bible he had brought off the sinking bomber.

And the one upon whose flopping hat the gull alighted when all were resigned to death from starvation, sunstroke and thirst.

Rick's control of himself even in such straits was such that, although he could not see the gull because the wilted brim of his hat hung over his eyes, he began to move his right hand so slowly up the lapel of his jacket and along the side of his drooping hat—while the other macabre men held their breaths and drooled—that the bird stayed on its strange perch. Then Rick's right hand sprang like a projectile. He seized the gull's spindly legs with a death grip, broke its neck with a swing or two and passed it around. The men and he gratefully sucked its blood, then plucked it swiftly and chewed its flesh and bones.

The miracle of the gull was a lifesaver, but transitory. Rick's problems soon beset him again. He lectured and relectured the men that they must not yield to the temptation to drink from the eternity of refreshing-looking sea water which surrounded them, no matter how thirst-crazed they were. He pulled back another dying man who was trying to drown himself, and excoriated him like an angry Prophet. Several of the B-17 crewmen in their abyss of despair cursed him as a latter-day Captain Bligh. Eddie alternated between cursing them back, and preaching to them from the New Testament: "If I take the wings of the morning, and dwell in the uttermost parts of the sea, even there shall Thy hand lead me, and Thy right hand shall hold me."

After twenty-four days and nights of incalculable horrors, they were sighted by search planes and rescued. Seven of the original eight had conquered the cruel sea. When he was put down safely on Canton for rehabilitation, Eddie's weight had dropped from 180 to 126. Army Air Force doctors and nurses brought his open sores under control, fattened him up a bit, and preparations were made to fly him and the others to the U.S. mainland to recuperate fully. But Captain Eddie, a stubborn soul, had other plans. He demanded and was flown to Australia, where he delivered his faded "eyes only" message to MacArthur.

Last time I saw Captain Eddie, not long before he died at eighty-two, he was steaming with anger when he arrived for our lunch at New York's "21" restaurant. His hat seemed a bit more crushed than normally, his suit was rain-stained, and there was a tear at knee level in one of his trouser legs. Rick ordered a double Bourbon to cool himself and collect his thoughts. Then he explained the extraordinary thing that had happened to him moments before—happened to a man who has weathered smashes against racetrack walls, bullets of the Red Baron, and plane crashes on land and sea: he had been advancing slowly through the revolving door of his office building when some burly and impatient young man entered the section behind him and gave it a mighty shove, propelling Eddie out onto the wet pavement like a diver plunging into a pool.

The fall stunned him momentarily. As he got up shakily and angrily, he saw his assailant escaping into the sidewalk crowd at full speed.

"If I could only have caught him," Rick said, finishing his drink but not his sentence. Then he shrugged, managed a smile, and added, "Ah, to be seventy again."

Ted Lawson, like the one hundred and forty other young Army Air Force officers and enlisted men, volunteered for what became known in military history as the Doolittle Raid without the foggiest idea of where he was going, what was expected of him, or why.

Their first briefing by Doolittle, by then back in uniform as a lieutenant colonel, was held behind locked doors at Eglin Field, near Pensacola, March 1, 1942. As for a clue about what they had gotten themselves into, Doolittle was about as informative as a clam.

"If you men have any idea that this isn't the most dangerous thing you've ever been on, don't even start the training period," began the man who had lived on danger. "You can drop out now. There isn't much sense wasting time and money training men who aren't going through with this thing. It's perfectly all right for any of you to drop out now."

Lawson's bride, a wonderful girl named Ellen, was pregnant. Another temptation to call off his volunteer role was that in recent months he had been assigned to routine air patrol against a possible Japanese attack on the West Coast. Such were the jitters of the pe-

riod following the bombing of Pearl Harbor. It was safe, easy duty
—except for a forced landing for fuel—and it kept him near Ellen.

But he and all the others remained silent in the wake of Doolittle's ominously brief call to arms.

One of his buddies spoke up and expressed the wish of all the
others for more details.

"I can't—just now," Doolittle said. "But you'll begin to get an
idea of what it's all about the longer we're down here training for
it. Now!—there's one important thing I want to stress. This whole
thing must be kept secret. I don't even want you to tell your wives,
no matter what you see or are asked to do down here. If you've
guessed where we're going, don't even talk about your guess. Don't
even talk among yourselves about this thing. Now, to repeat, does
anybody want to drop out?"

Nobody dropped out.

Several crews subsequently dropped out after getting no answers
to their questions as to why they were being asked to take their
fifteen-ton B-25 medium bombers off marked portions of Eglin's
long runways—some of the markings being hardly 400 feet—but
were not asked to return and land within the same cramped
confines. The fact that Navy carrier pilots were their chief instruc-
tors during those practice takeoffs meant little to the crews that
chose to return to a war they understood.

Lawson and his crew did not fully comprehend the outrageous
nature of the mission until ordered, early in April of 1942, to make
a low-level flight across the country from Eglin to Alameda, California, and to taxi to the pier where the carrier *Hornet* was berthed.
Once at sea, their B-25s huddled and chained on the rear half of the
Hornet's deck, the crews finally heard the true word from Doolittle: they were going to throw the first counterpunch against Japan
since Pearl Harbor, five months earlier. The *Hornet* and the task
force assigned to protect them would get them as close to Japan as
feasible, possibly as close as 400 miles. They would then be expected
to take off from the 400 feet of the *Hornet*'s forward deck with four
500-pound bombs, fly low and slow (166 mph) to the enemy's land,
come in very low to avoid radar detection, rise to 1,500 feet over

their appointed targets, bomb, and then hope to reach emergency fields on the China mainland. Aside from Tokyo, the main drop, there would be smaller attacks on Yokohama, Osaka, Kobe and Nagoya.

They got a bad break. The task force was spotted by a Japanese trawler about 800 miles off Japan on the morning of April 18, 1942. It had to be presumed that before being sunk—which it was in a hurry—the trawler had sent a radio warning to Tokyo that a considerable U.S. attack force was on the way. A hard decision had to be made on the spot. It was originally intended to advance at full speed through the day, launch the bombers after dark, and bomb under cover of night. Toward that end an intrepid Navy submarine crew had slipped into Tokyo Bay and, at great risk, made observations of the positions of the captive balloons and their long steel tethers which were designed to snare and destroy any low-flying enemy aircraft. Doolittle's B-25, scheduled to be first off the deck of the *Hornet,* was loaded with a ton of incendiary bombs, "to light up the targets." They had to be replaced with conventional bombs, extra gas tanks were strapped in the cramped bombers, and flight plans and patterns were revised. It could have been a panic situation, but every plane managed to take off the plunging deck in the teeth of a 30-knot, rainswept gale.

The rest of the epic has been chronicled in books, films, and documentaries, and has become part of the folklore of war. All sixteen bombers were lost after performing their missions over Japan. One flew on to Vladivostok after dropping its bombs, and the Russians—not then at war with Japan—interned it and its crew. The fifteen other planes, whose crews had anticipated reaching the emergency fields on the China Coast at dawn, arrived in the area of the refueling strips around midnight—because of their premature takeoff from the carrier. The fields, of course, were not lighted. Japanese occupation units were scattered over the general area, having been alerted to be on the lookout for the Americans. With their engines running out of fuel after the long escape route from Japan, some of the B-25 crews bailed out; others chose to take a chance on ditching as near to land as possible. None could have given too much thought at the time to the fact that they had altered the course of the war, had demonstrated to confident Japanese warlords that their homeland could indeed be reached by an adversary, and the future augured worse.

Prowling Japanese patrols captured two crews. Three of the ten American airmen were executed before firing squads, after flimsy and internationally illegal trials. A fourth died of malnutrition. The remaining six somehow weathered untold anguish and torture until that distant day called V-J. One of these, Corporal Jacob, who later said that a voice had sustained him as he was dying of starvation, studied for the ministry after the war and is now a missionary in Japan.

Of the wounded who escaped capture, Lawson was the worst off. Both engines quit on him as he eased his B-25, forebodingly named "The Ruptured Duck," toward the beach of a small island off the China Coast. His hope was to make a safe landing on the beach, wait out the night, then try to take off at daybreak and find the emergency strip. Instead, with no power left to continue his approach to the beach, he was forced to ditch. The smash against the water was so violent that Lawson was catapulted through the bomber's narrow windshield, still strapped to his ripped-out seat.

The next thing he remembered was sitting under water, filled with a sense of peace. He was drowning, he suddenly realized as if a bolt of lightning had penetrated his euphoria. He clawed open his seat belt and shoulder harness, pulled the handles that shot gas into his Mae West, and floated to the angry surface more dead than alive. The waves rolled him to the beach. He did not know that his left leg had been ripped open from his thigh to his boot.

Friendly Chinese guerrillas found him on the beach that ghastly night, his face flattened, most of his teeth gone, and his leg bleeding badly. Over the next few days and nights they carried him by makeshift litter and small riverboat to the mainland, where the threat of capture by the Japanese was increased, and on to a primitive Chinese hospital. Lawson's battered crew, all still ambulatory, followed at his side. There wasn't even an aspirin to share.

Providentially, another B-25 crew that was "walking out" after parachuting to safety, was led to the same little hospital. It included the only doctor among the original eighty men on the raid—Lieutenant Ed White—and the only reason he had been accepted as a participant was that he had previously won a rating as a machine gunner.

Lawson's crew and the crew of which Doc White had been a member moved on. White stayed with Lawson, whose condition was worsening, and told him the bad news: he would have to amputate the leg.

Men of guts never are unnecessarily wordy. Lawson remembered the basic dialogue later in his book *Thirty Seconds Over Tokyo.**

"I said to Doc that I guessed it wouldn't be so bad, with it off. It would be something like wearing a shoe with a high instep. I waited, but Doc didn't answer, and for the first time I knew he was going to take more than my foot and ankle. I told him I wanted to be sure he took it off well below the knee.

"Doc was busy thinking about something else. He still didn't answer, so I had to come out and ask him *where* he'd take it off.

" 'Well,' Doc said, 'above the knee. I'll leave you as much as I can.' " (A Chinese intern had jogged for most of two days and nights previously to a larger village to fetch and bring back the spinal anesthetic without which Ted could not have survived.)

"Doc took his time, after the spinal shot. I told him I thought the leg was dead. He wanted to be sure. But at last he came over to the table with a scalpel in his hand. I cocked an eye down as he started but I couldn't see any blood or feel anything. But I knew he was cutting. I could see his arm moving and see him lift my leg up so he could cut underneath.

"Now I felt that I could move the toes of my good leg and it worried me. I thought the anesthetic must be wearing off. I told Doc I could move my whole right ankle now. Two Chinese nurses came up on either side of the table and held my wrists. Doc stepped away and walked back quickly with a saw. It made a strange, faraway, soggy sound as he sawed through the bone.

*Random House, 1943.

"Then there was an almost musical twink, and deep, deep silence inside me as Doc laid aside the saw. The Chinese nurses let go of my wrists . . ."

At an American-run hostel in Kweilin one night, during the long and painful voyage home, someone asked Lawson, "You think it was worthwhile?"

"I thought it over for a time, trying to see the whole thing objectively," Ted wrote later. "When I finally said that I did think it was worthwhile, I meant it. We'll probably never know just how much damage we caused. The important thing, I figured, was that our people back home got a lift out of it. It made them sure that one day we could really go to work on the Japanese, no matter how far away they were.

"I hadn't thought much about our people before that. A fellow doesn't volunteer for something like the Japan raid, bomb the place, try to get away, and in my case lose a leg, and say, 'This is for the dear people.' You just don't say or feel those things. You think about yourself most of the time: whether you'll have guts enough to go through with the thing, and whether you'll get away with it. It's only later, when you add things up and get the sum, that you think of the people. And the cause. And then you hope you've done both of them some good."

Chapter 14

*If you outdrive me once more I'm gonna lift up your skirt and
make sure you're a girl.*

GEORGE HERMAN RUTH (1895–1948) during a charity
golf match against Mildred Ella Didrikson Zaharias
(1914–1956)

Yes, America had two immortal Babes. There was the fat guy from
Baltimore who set home-run and pitching records that lasted a generation and more, and then there was the trim tomboy from Texas.
No baseball player before or since ever equaled Babe as a Man For
All Seasons (and positions). No girl athlete could ever do muscular
things as varied or as well as The Other Babe, rawboned as a broncobuster, tender as a member of the Vassar daisy-chain gang. I
revered him, loved her.

Babe Didrikson came up the hard way. One of seven children of
a Norwegian cabinetmaker, next to the youngest and called Baby,
she changed her nickname in a curious way. Whenever her brothers
went off to play baseball she tagged along, insisted on playing, and
began hitting the ball with the vigor and distance that reminded
friend and foe of the prowess of the immortal star of the New York
Yankees. Hence: Babe instead of Baby.

As a kid she worked like a slavey, first in an Italian grocery
store after school, and then in a fig-packing plant. At night, when
lessons were finished, her father Ole, who had become a great sports
fan, briefed the children on the sports news of the day by reading
from his newspaper. In time, he built them a gym and dreamed of
their becoming athletic stars. Babe was particularly ignited by his
dreams.

"Next year I'm going to win the Olympics myself," she swore
after her father had read an account of the Amsterdam Games of
1928. She was fourteen.

"You'll have to wait four years," Ole mildly reminded her. "They don't hold the Games every year."

She didn't wait that long to startle U.S. sports fans. At sixteen, while working as a stenographer for the Employers Casualty Company of Beaumont, Texas, she was urged by an insurance man named M. J. McCombs to enter the 1930 Women's National A.A.U. Track and Field Championships in Dallas. She won five titles and for several delirious minutes was the holder of a sixth, the world's record in the broad jump—until a much-better-known performer, Stella Walsh, outjumped her by the margin of a quarter of an inch.

Babe became a world figure in the 1932 Olympics at Los Angeles. She entered three events. She won the Olympic Gold Medal for her javelin thrust of 143 feet, $3^{11}\!/_{16}$ inches, and a second Gold Medal for lowering her already-held U.S. record to 11.7 in the 80-meter hurdles. (She had rehearsed for that one by soaring over the hedges that separated the front yards of her block in Beaumont.) There was a storm of controversy when Olympic officials disqualified her in the high-jump event because she *dived* over the bar—long since a standard practice. Their decision cost her a third Olympic Gold Medal.

Something happened to her a few days after the L. A. Olympics that in time was to change her life and the role of women in sports in general. A few of the most renowned sportswriters of that time— Grantland Rice, Westbrook Pegler, Paul Gallico and Braven Dyer, all of whom had watched and admired her in the Games—invited her to accompany them to the Brentwood (California) Golf and Country Club, for kicks. They had arranged a foursome, but thought it might be amusing to have a great girl athlete—who had never been on a golf course—as their gallery.

It is still not quite clear as to which one of the four, none of them much better than hackers, with the exception of Rice, suggested to the club pro, Olin Dutra, that he give a short lesson to Babe in how to swing a wood. The lesson is said to have lasted nearly two minutes. Then, after the tame foursome had teed off, it was suggested that Babe try to hit one off the first tee.

She did. It sailed and rolled 240 yards down the middle of the fairway.

The saga of Babe Didrikson, the golfer, should have begun then and there in 1932. But it didn't. To help the family income she embarked on a rough-and-tumble career as a professional in basketball —only girl on the team, of course, and subject to all the bumps, bruises and bloody noses of that trade. Once, in the tawdry gym at George Washington University in Washington, D.C., I covered a game in which she clutched the bull neck of All-America football star Jim Bausch with a stranglehold he couldn't break, even by spinning her around and around, airborne.

Today, a top girl star in tennis or golf can gross as much as the salary of the President of the United States. But not during the Great Depression. Babe was known to pitch for the bearded House of David semipro ball club for fifty dollars a game. The public image of her after her Olympic triumphs and her earthy efforts to help support her family was hardly encouraging. She offered her services to pro football, wrestling and boxing promoters. They laughed at her. She wore her hair like young men did in those days —manly. She wore slacks at a time when nice girls didn't, preferred men's shirts open at the neck instead of feminine blouses. Her gossiping inferiors said she was a lesbian.

But Babe was wonderfully feminine underneath a surface many found tough. And she was lonely. In her solitude, when the din of a cheap game in loutish surroundings was over, and she had some time off, the greatest girl athlete of all time would repair to her electric grill and cook fine meals for an imaginary husband, try on a frilly dress she would never think of wearing in public, knit, or play mournful tunes on the mouth organ she always carried with her.

When Babe took up golf seriously, she shed all the trashier sports of her life and competed as an amateur. She would spend as many as twelve hours a day on a course, taking lessons or playing, and carry home books by golf masters to read at night, or rules to memorize. In 1935 she won her first tournament, the Texas State Women's Amateur title at River Oaks, Houston. Babe won the key hole of the match late in the day. Her opponent and tournament favorite, Peggy Chandler, was the best woman golfer of that time and had dropped a long putt for a birdie on a difficult par-5 hole. Babe kept her head down, swung into the rough with a wedge Gene Sarazen had given her, and holed out for an eagle!

A man came into her life: George Zaharias, the huge professional wrestler who was billed during his prime as "The Crying Greek from Cripple Creek." He was, by far, the most ferocious-looking matman of his time. But, like Babe, this son of a Greek steelworker named Vetoyanis was a sentimental soul beneath the hard-looking surface.

"Rassling George is quite an experience," the late Herman Hickman, All-America at Tennessee, wrestler and football coach at Yale, once told me. "For all his grunts, growls and yells, it's like making love to a tender fat lady."

When Babe and George were married in 1937, a flippant New York sportswriter called it "a case of love at first fright."

But it was love at first sight, actually. George was invited to a tournament in which Babe was playing and, after sampling this group and that, found himself following Babe's foursome. For two or three holes, George walked beside her like a huge bodyguard. Then he fell directly behind her, "so I could admire the way she moved," he told me years later. "I had fallen in love with her. After we were married, when I looked at her, she was the most beautiful girl I ever saw. I'm downright ugly, like you know, but Babe would look at me and say, 'George, you're beautiful; you're just the most beautiful man I ever did see.' She believed it, really believed it . . . and I would believe it, too."

(Making people feel good was part of Babe's character. I played with her once in a practice round before she starred in the Washington *Post* Pro-Am tournament at Columbia Country Club. On one hole, which she was playing perfectly, I sliced into a hostile sand trap. Babe walked up the fairway ahead of me and the other members of the foursome. I noticed vaguely that she went into the trap that imprisoned my ball and then carefully raked her spike prints. I wondered why. She was on the fairway fifty yards or so beyond my marooned hit. But as soon as I reached the trap, I knew why she had gone in there. She had teed up my ball on a six-inch tee.)

George had saved his money, which meant that Babe, for the first time since she was a child, was not obliged to work. But she worked for George, helped him set up a golf club in Tampa and run a ranch in Colorado, and kept improving her golf. Through 1946–47 she won seventeen consecutive amateur women's titles, including the U.S. and British Opens, the first time the latter had been accomplished. Something of an international crisis rose when Babe appeared in slacks in the latter event, too . . . an unprecedented vision in the discreet realm of British women's golf annals. But there was no official objection. She had had them tailored in the clan plaid of the governor of the club, and he was immensely pleased. Back in New York, Babe was given a rare ticker-tape parade up Broadway.

The Zahariases had it made, except a secret sorrow they never talked about. Babe had lost two prematurely-born babies, a boy and a girl. There is no way to describe how much she wanted them. But life went on. Their club at Tampa prospered, she became a professional, and her name adorned golf clubs, golf outfits, and all the other fringe benefits of the rapidly expanding women's game. In 1950 the Associated Press bestowed on her a climactic award. It named her the Greatest Female Athlete of the Half Century. She was crowned in good company: the Greatest Male Athlete of the Half Century was the legendary Jim Thorpe.

In 1953 an unexplainable shadow fell over Babe. She began to tire badly in the late rounds of tournaments—she of all persons. Finally, after winning the Babe Zaharias Open at Beaumont, she went alone to the office of an old family friend, Dr. W. E. Tatum. The white-haired, eighty-year-old specialist examined her at length. Babe watched his face in the oppressive silence of the examination room. It was she who broke the silence.

"I've got cancer, haven't I?" she said.

Her old friend's answer was a nod, and tears.

She called George.

"We'll fight it together," he said, with a show of robustness. "I'll be with you every minute."

The night before the operation by Dr. Robert M. Moore, Chairman of the Department of Surgery in the John Sealey Division of the University of Texas Medical School, Babe was tense and restless.

"You're going to win this one, Babe," George told her, massaging her legs. "And when you win it, people all over the world are going to take heart and lose some of their fear of cancer. Just stay loose, Babe."

Babe cheered up. "Honey, do me a favor," she said. "I want you to get my golf clubs and put them in the corner of my room. I'm going to use them again."

The bag of golf clubs was the first thing Babe's eyes focused on when she was brought back to her room after the colostomy, which rerouted her cancerous intestinal tract. When she was able to leave her bed she would sometimes make it across the room to her clubs and touch them, even waggle them a bit. After a month she made a daily tour of the hospital, sometimes dipping into a pocket for her harmonica. Seventy days after the operation, she walked out of the hospital on George's arm, still a bit shaky but ready to take on the world once more.

A month later, she stepped up to the first tee at the Tam O'Shanter Country Club (Niles, Illinois) before a huge bated-breath gallery and drove the ball "a country mile" down the middle. It was the beginning of a comeback that will live forever in sports. Its culmination came at the Salem Country Club (Peabody, Massachusetts) in 1954. On that 6,398-yard course, with a men's par of 72, Babe shot rounds of 72, 71, 73 and 75 to win the U. S. Women's Open by twelve strokes. It was the thirty-third tournament she had won since turning pro.

In April 1955, before the opening of what everyone assumed would be another successful season, Babe hurt herself in a unique manner. During a vacation at a Texas beach her Ford station wagon became stuck in the sand. Babe did what came naturally, for her. She clamped a grip on the rear bumper and tried to *lift* it out of its predicament. The effort slipped a disc in her straight Norwegian back. She ignored the pain and over the next two months played in three tournaments, winning one of them. But it became too much of a grind, even for Babe. So she returned to John Sealey and was operated on by Dr. Samuel B. Snodgrass.

Months later, when her back was strong again, there was something new, a dull pain in her strong but graceful legs. She took her problem to Dr. Grace Jameson of the John Sealey staff. When all the tests were completed, Babe asked the question.

"What is it this time?"

The two professionals, golf and medicine, looked into each other's eyes.

"Babe," Dr. Jameson said, "the X rays show that it's cancer again."

Dr. Jameson explained to the stoic sports champion that this time it was cancer of the sacrum, a triangular-shaped bone at the back of the pelvis and base of the spine. Through the sacrum's openings thread the nerves that lead from the endless muscles of the legs to the brain. Cancer had formed in these vents, pinching the nerves and producing what Dr. Jameson later told me "must have been excruciating pain."

"What'll we do about it?" Babe quietly asked the doctor who had given her the stunning news that her colostomy had not stopped the spread.

"X-ray therapy," Dr. Jameson replied.

"Well, let's get going," said Babe.

The sacrum was bombarded with rays for weeks. But there are limits to such treatment. When it became inadvisable to continue, Dr. Snodgrass performed a five-and-a-half-hour cordotomy on Babe. It is a nerve-severing operation designed to block the processes which inform the brain of the existence of pain. It was done on Friday the thirteenth, July 1956.

I flew to Galveston to see her, when she was able to receive visitors. George drove me to the hospital. The hospital's Muzak was softly playing "Greensleeves" as we entered Babe's cool, darkened room. I've always found it almost too melancholy to hear, even a chant of impending doom.

Babe lay under a sheet. The room was filled with gifts of a religious nature. There were no golf clubs standing in the corner.

"It was a long, tough one," she told me wanly, "but thank the good Lord it killed the pain." She adjusted a cold cloth over most of her face.

"All I feel now is something here in my chest, but they tell me that'll go away soon. My legs were killing me for weeks, but I don't feel a thing down there now. Funny thing, I don't even know how long they are, though the reflexes seem okay."

A nurse heated a hypodermic needle over a match and, on muted instructions from Babe, walked around the bed and gave it to her in the left arm. The legs that had leaped to new heights in the Olympics, jumped about basketball courts from coast to coast, run out hits in exhibition baseball games (she once struck out Joe DiMaggio), and marched to victory in fifty-six major golf tournaments here and abroad, stirred slowly beneath the sheet.

"I can move them okay," Babe said sleepily. "See? My arms, too. But I just can't eat, doggone it. I'm so doggone weak I can't even boost my bottom off the bed. But shucks, soon as I start eating I'll be okay. I'll be up and out of here . . ."

"You sure will, honey," George rumbled from his chair nearby.

Babe dozed, and George and I tiptoed into the hall.

"I don't know how to say it good," he said, low-voiced. "All I know is that when she hurts, I hurt. I wake up at night feeling that something isn't right with her. 'Go home, George,' the nurse says. 'Get some sleep. She's comfortable.' But I know she's not. So I sit there and watch her. Sometimes she must be dreaming that she's back in our garden in Tampa. You hear her say, like she was talking to the gardener, 'Ed, please put the roses over there.' And she plays golf at night. Her fingers work, gripping the club she's dreaming about. I don't know how to say it . . ."

As we strolled along the corridor half a dozen scampering nurses or slowly moving patients asked, "How's Babe?" George said, "She's coming along just fine, thanks." A patient laughed as he told George that he had heard that Babe asked her nurse to get her the papers, and quoted Babe as saying, "I want to see how I feel."

We dropped in on Dr. Jameson.

"She has so much fight in her that I marvel," she said. "She constantly puts herself aside, inquires about other patients, asks about my four children."

Dr. Moore, the first to operate on Babe for cancer, shook his head in wonderment. "She's worried over a slight game leg of mine," he said. "She won't talk to me about it when I see her. But I know she asks the other doctors and the nurses about me. Imagine."

Dr. John Otto, neurologist and psychiatrist, had a word about the remarkable patient, too.

"She's one of those you can tell the truth to," he said. "George tells me that after they had wept a bit over the news that the cancer hadn't been caught, she said, 'You can cry just so long, and then you have to stop and think things out. We've cried enough, George; let's get the house in order.'"

I went back to Babe's room the next day. She was drugged but in good spirits.

"Ask me anything you want to," she said with a shadow of her familiar grin. "But don't write me off, Buster. Look, the old legs are as good as ever." She moved them under the bedclothes as if pedaling a bicycle. The effort obviously exhausted her.

"I don't want to ask you anything, Baby," I said, bending over her to kiss her on the cheek. "I just came by to say I love you."

Chapter 15

. . . good, the more Communicated,
more abundant grows . . .
JOHN MILTON (1608–1674)

On the back of an envelope found among his effects after his death in a plane crash, former Atomic Energy Commission chairman Gordon Dean had scribbled:

LESSONS LEARNED

1—Never lose your capacity for enthusiasm.

2—Never lose your capacity for indignation.

3—Never judge people, don't type them too quickly; but in a pinch never first assume that a man is bad; first assume always that he is good and that at worst he is in the gray area between bad and good.

4—Never be impressed by wealth alone or thrown by poverty.

5—If you can't be generous when it's hard to be, you won't be when it's easy.

6—The greatest builder of confidence is the ability to do something —almost anything—well.

7—When that confidence comes, then strive for humility; you aren't as good as all that.

8—And the way to become truly useful is to seek the best that other brains have to offer. Use them to supplement your own, and be prepared to give credit to them when they have helped.

9—The greatest tragedies in world and personal events stem from misunderstandings.

ANSWER: communicate.

So, meet a communicator. And his wife, the inventor of a communications system that might have baffled or discouraged Samuel F. B. Morse, Alexander Graham Bell, Guglielmo Marconi and Aleksandr Popov. They are Corbin and Kay Allerdice, parents of three sons. Allerdice was one of the bright young men of the Atomic Energy Commission and, later, the World Bank. He couldn't miss in that league of intellectuals.

Then, a strange thing. One afternoon while at work at the World Bank headquarters in Washington, Allerdice detected what he easily identified as a common sniffly cold coming on. He told his secretary that he was going to knock off work early, go home, take a couple of aspirins, go to bed . . . and he'd be in early the next morning.

He couldn't wake up the next morning. Kay called their doctor, their doctor called a neurologist. The neurologist determined that Allerdice had been stricken by a massive virus attack on his central nervous system.

For weeks, the animated young official lay flat on his back, eyes closed, unable to speak, fed intravenously. He was a faintly breathing dead man, a quadraplegic.

One day he opened his eyes. The smallest muscles in his body, those that activate the eyelids, had somehow been reborn. Kay, who had kept the lonely vigils, bounded from her chair at the side of his bed and stood at its foot, the better to watch the face of her husband. She looked into his opened eyes, twin pools of doubt, wonder, even despair.

"Hello, Corb," she said. There was no response, no reaction. He looked at her unblinkingly.

A miraculous thought came to her in her terrible anxiety to get through to him. "Corb," she said, "I want to see if you know me. If you know me, tell me by blinking your eyes. Blink your eyes, Corb. Now."

Allerdice blinked his eyes and, overcome with gratitude that his brain still lived, the good wife set out to devise means of utilizing that simple action of his eyes to establish a rapport with the mute and graven man.

She found it.

"Tell you what," she said one day. "I know there must be a lot of things you want to say to me. So let's try this: I'm going to recite the alphabet, over and over and over. You keep your eyes open while I'm doing it. When I get to a letter which is part of a word you want me to know, you blink your eyes and I'll write it down. And sooner or later, I'll know what you're saying to me."

By that excruciatingly tedious method the Allerdices found communion once more. In time, after her countless recitations of the alphabet, he communicated the news that some sense of feeling had returned to a couple of fingers on his right hand. He had a request or two. He wanted his typewriter wheeled to the side of his bed, a pulley built to support his hand over the keyboard, and to be rolled on his side so that he could see the keys. That took days, probably weeks.

But when all was attended to, Allerdice was able to touch, not really depress, the letters of the words he wanted to transmit, while Kay looked over his shoulder. It speeded up their communication a hundredfold.

Later, two engineer friends designed a novel system that mated an electric typewriter with a clear screen which fit over his bed like a combination of a dinner tray and windshield. When Allerdice touched a key the letter would light up on the screen, backward for the man in bed, frontward for those visitors who sat or stood at the bottom of his bed.

Now he could address himself to groups, not just the faithful wife counting and recording the blinking of his eyes. He could carry on not only modest "conversations" but participate in debates. To save him the trouble of spelling out his dissent, if the one-sided talk concerned a political issue, say, Corbin's wizard friends wired up a rasping disapproval button.

Allerdice went the distance at Dr. Howard Rusk's remarkable rehabilitation center at Bellevue Hospital in New York City, where a host of stricken celebrities, including Joseph P. Kennedy, Sr., sire of the remarkable and ill-starred clan, Roy Campanella, one of the great baseball catchers of his time, and Jim Hagerty, President Eisenhower's press secretary, fought to rise above it.

For the past few years, Allerdice has been confined to the Newton D. Baker Veterans Hospital, Martinsburg, West Virginia. He has kept himself busy by writing a history of the Atomic Energy Commission and the remarkable personnel which produced the first A-bomb. Praeger Publishers have recently distributed it to college libraries as one of a series on government departments and agencies. Corb was helped and encouraged in his efforts by his friend Edward R. Trapnell, with whom he worked at AEC.

"We worked on the book over a period of five years, but Corb kept plugging away despite the fact that I sometimes couldn't work on it with him for weeks at a time because of job pressures and a heart attack I had in 1971. Corb is still brave and bright, his mind sharp. He punches an electric typewriter (using a roll of paper) at a rate of about five to seven punches a minute . . ."

That is not going to break the late Billy Rose's record for speed-typing, but Allerdice has achieved a miracle Rose and a zillion other better-known inhabitants of this globe have stumbled over, for one reason and another.

Corbin Allerdice has communicated.

So can you.